IT HAPPENED TO ME

Series Editor: Arlene Hirschfelder

Books in the It Happened To Me series are designed for inquisitive teens digging for answers about certain illnesses, social issues, or lifestyle interests. Whether you are deep into your teen years or just entering them, these books are gold mines of up-to-date information, riveting teen views, and great visuals to help you figure out stuff. Besides special boxes highlighting singular facts, each book is enhanced with the latest reading list, websites, and an index. Perfect for browsing, there's loads of expert information by acclaimed writers to help parents, guardians, and librarians understand teen illness, tough situations, and lifestyle choices.

1. *Learning Disabilities: The Ultimate Teen Guide,* by Penny Hutchins Paquette and Cheryl Gerson Tuttle, 2003.
2. *Epilepsy: The Ultimate Teen Guide,* by Kathlyn Gay and Sean McGarrahan, 2002.
3. *Stress Relief: The Ultimate Teen Guide,* by Mark Powell, 2002.
4. *Making Sexual Decisions: The Ultimate Teen Guide,* by L. Kris Gowen, Ph.D., 2003.
5. *Asthma: The Ultimate Teen Guide,* by Penny Hutchins Paquette, 2003.
6. *Cultural Diversity: Conflicts and Challenges: The Ultimate Teen Guide,* by Kathlyn Gay, 2003.
7. *Diabetes: The Ultimate Teen Guide,* by Katherine J. Moran, 2004.
8. *When Will I Stop Hurting? Teens, Loss, and Grief: The Ultimate Teen Guide,* by Edward Myers, 2004.

When Will I Stop Hurting?

Teens, Loss, and Grief

EDWARD MYERS

ILLUSTRATIONS BY KELLY ADAMS

It Happened to Me, No. 8

The Scarecrow Press, Inc.
Lanham, Maryland • Toronto • Oxford
2004

SCARECROW PRESS, INC.

Published in the United States of America
by Scarecrow Press, Inc.
A wholly owned subsidary of The Rowman & Littlefield Publishing Group, Inc.
4501 Forbes Boulevard, Suite 200, Lanham, Maryland 20706
www.scarecrowpress.com

PO Box 317
Oxford
OX2 9RU, UK

British Library Cataloguing in Publication Information Available

Library of Congress Cataloging-in-Publication Data

Myers, Edward, 1950–
 When will I stop hurting? : teens, loss, and grief / Edward
Myers ; illustrations by Kelly Adams.
  p. cm. — (It happened to me ; no. 8)
  Includes bibliographical references and index.
  ISBN 0-8108-4921-6 (alk. paper)
 1. Bereavement in adolescence—Psychological aspects. 2.
Grief in adolescence. 3. Loss (Psychology) in adolescence. I. Title.
II. Series
BF724.3.G73 M94 2004
155.9'37'0835—dc22

                                        2003023698

∞™ The paper used in this publication meets the minimum requirements of
American National Standard for Information Sciences—Permanence of Paper
for Printed Library Materials, ANSI/NISO Z39.48-1992.
Manufactured in the United States of America.

Contents

85.888

Introduction

Grief is the price we pay for love.

If you love someone and that person dies, you'll be hit hard by the loss. The emotions you feel may differ from what other people feel—grief is a profoundly individual experience. But just as you have loved, you will grieve.

This situation is hard—one of life's hardest realities—but it's what we face as human beings. There's no point in pretending otherwise. Although modern American culture often goes to great lengths to ignore death and its effects on the living, grief is unavoidable. Grief, as the English author C. S. Lewis stated, "is a universal and integral part of our experience of love."[1]

You're probably reading this book because someone you love has died. Or maybe someone is seriously ill. You're feeling some painful, confusing emotions about what's happening. You want to understand these feelings and make sense of them. You want to ease your pain.

I sympathize with your situation because I've been there, too. By the age of twenty, I'd experienced the loss of all four of my grandparents, two friends, and a brother. My father died shortly after that, and my mother a few years later. I know what grief is, and I know it's hard. I'm sorry if you're dealing with your own losses.

But the great likelihood is that you'll cope with these difficult experiences, adjust to your loss, and become a stronger, wiser person as a consequence. No one can make grief simply disappear. No one can make grief painless. Yet I can assure you of one thing: if you can understand grief and its effects on you,

you'll have an easier time adjusting to what has happened and coping with the complex, intense emotions typical of the grief process.

That's why I've written this book.

Here's a quick overview of *When Will I Stop Hurting?*

Chapter 1, "Tales of Loss and Grief," presents a wide range of teenagers' stories (in the teens' own words) about the losses they've experienced. Later chapters include quotes from many teens about specific issues they've confronted during the course of bereavement.

Chapter 2, "The Nature of Grief and Bereavement," provides an initial description of what grief is, what happens throughout the grief process, what emotions are typical, and how long this process typically lasts.

After these introductory sections, chapters 3 and 4 offer more detail about the nature of grief. Chapter 3, "Kinds of Loss," explains how the aftermath of a sudden death differs from the aftermath of a prolonged illness. Chapter 4, "Other Ways Loss and Grief Can Affect You," describes some of the personal and family consequences of losing someone you love.

Chapters 5 and 6 then provide a wide range of suggestions for how to help yourself during bereavement. These aren't "cure-alls"—grief will take a while to diminish, and nothing can make the process happen fast or without a lot of patience. But you can take many steps to ease your pain.

Chapter 7, "Warning Signs," describes some issues to monitor. Grief is a normal process of adjusting to loss, and most people go through the experience without serious problems. But it's good to keep an eye out for a few issues that can signal complications.

Finally, chapter 8 offers concluding thoughts about loss and grief in the words of teenagers, writers, and bereavement experts.

There's also a resource guide that includes information about service agencies, books, and websites that may be helpful as you cope with grief.

I'm aware that what we're talking about here is a heavy subject. None of what follows is "light reading." What I'm hoping, however, is that if you've experienced a loss, these discussions will be useful.

I wish you well.

NOTES

1. C. S. Lewis, *A Grief Observed* (San Francisco: Harper San Francisco, 2001), 37.

Tales of Loss and Grief

None of the following stories is long or detailed; each one is simply a teenager's brief comments about a loss that he or she has suffered. The reason I'm quoting these stories is to show both the variety of loss and what teenagers experience during grief. I hope that what these teens have been through helps you realize that your own feelings are normal—that they are feelings you share with many other people.

Feel free to pick and choose among these stories, selecting some to read while ignoring others. Follow your own hunches about what applies to your own situation and what doesn't.

DEATH OF A PARENT

The death of a parent hits most teenagers especially hard. Losing your mother or father leaves you dealing with many complex emotional and practical issues. If you were close to your parent, then you'll grieve the loss of a warm, nurturing relationship. But even if you weren't close to your parent, his or her death can affect you intensely, as you'll be left with unresolved conflicts and misunderstandings. For almost all teens, the death of a parent changes many dynamics within the family, and it may also complicate aspects of your personal

Life changes forever when a parent dies.
—Earl A. Grollman, American grief expert and rabbi[1]

1

situation—where you live, whom you live with, where you attend school, and other issues.

Arielle, Late Teens

My mom had been sick for as long as I could remember. She'd been diagnosed as having lupus erythmatosis when I was four, and ever since then she'd been sick. Sometimes she could function pretty well. Other times she was bedridden. At times she went to the hospital for days or even weeks. My dad coped fairly well but worked at his job all day and then took care of me and my brother and sister in the afternoon and evening. What amazes me is somehow they kept going. Even my mother. I have no idea how she raised three children while dealing with all her health problems.

What I remember most is that she always seemed tired. She was in her forties when I was a teenager but looked and acted much, much older. When she came to school for class visits or assemblies, some of the other kids would ask me if she was my grandmother. That was hard. She also couldn't do a lot of things the other mothers did. She felt terrible most of the time and she had no energy. Sometimes she got very impatient with us kids and ordered us around. She cried a lot. Not in front of us—in another room. But I knew she felt frustrated and sad about being sick. I think my brother and sister and I tried to help her somewhat—we all did chores—but we didn't really know what to do that would make a difference.

We just wanted to be ordinary kids. I didn't invite other kids over to my house because I felt afraid they'd be grossed out or maybe they'd make fun of me because my mother was an invalid. I felt bad about that, but all I really wanted was a normal life.

One day my mother went off to the hospital. Later that week my dad told me she was very, very sick. My aunt was looking after us at home. Nobody really told us much about what was happening, but somehow I knew something was different. We visited her and she looked awful.

I remember lying on my bed and worrying about Mom. It was early autumn—warm outside—and my window was open.

There was a big tree right outside my window, and a whole lot of birds were roosting in that tree. They were chirping like crazy! Then, suddenly, they stopped—all of them. They fell totally silent. I looked outside because the silence startled me. I checked the clock: five thirty-one.

A few hours later, Dad came home and told us kids that Mom had passed away that afternoon. I asked him when. He said, "Just a minute or so after five thirty."

Michael, College Age

During my sophomore year at college I was nineteen and living in New York City. I spoke with my parents frequently by phone. In April, right before spring break, I called them to make plans for coming home to Chicago. My mom sounded upset when I phoned—my dad was sick. He'd caught the flu, or something, and had severe headaches. A day or so later he was still sick. This was unusual—Dad almost never got sick. But Mom said he'd been to the doctor and it was just the flu, nothing serious. Then a day later Dad was even sicker, with more headaches and some difficulties with his vision. That was about the time I was scheduled to head home for the break, so I thought, "Well, Mom will take care of him and I'll see him soon."

But when I arrived at O'Hare, my aunt Judy met me there. She said, "Your dad is in intensive care and isn't expected to make it through the day." I couldn't believe it. I asked her what the heck was going on, and she said, "He's had a severe stroke." It was a cerebral hemorrhage. They'd already done surgery on him, but he'd been bleeding in his brain and was now paralyzed. So we raced to the hospital.

He died a few hours later. I never got to see him alive—the doctors worked on him the whole time, and then suddenly he went into cardiac arrest. So the surgeon came out and said to Mom, "I'm sorry to tell you this, but your husband just died."

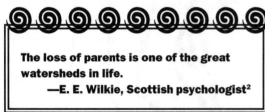

The loss of parents is one of the great watersheds in life.
—E. E. Wilkie, Scottish psychologist[2]

I couldn't believe it. I'd talked with him just a few days before that. He was such a big, healthy man. Now suddenly he was gone. It made no sense. How could somebody who was so alive now be dead? But he was.

I'd always been so close to him. . . . Just a week or two earlier I'd been talking with a friend about our parents, and she didn't get along too well with hers, and I'd said, "I can't imagine how I'd ever keep going if my parents died—especially my dad." And now he was dead.

Nikki, Mid-Teens

My mom died suddenly from a massive heart attack. It was a total surprise to everyone. We had no idea she had any problems with her heart. Afterwards I was in shock and disbelief. She died eight days before Christmas. I was numb throughout Christmas. I didn't feel anything at first then it hit me—*she was gone*. I coped with the situation by going to school for JROTC practices. We had some throughout Christmas vacation.

Time is the only comforter for the loss of a mother.
—Jane Welsh Carlyle, Scottish writer[3]

Janice, Mid-Teens

The most difficult part of my father's death is growing up without him. You see, I had my father wrapped around my little finger since the moment I was conceived. In a way I felt guilty for this, but I hurt more for him than my grandmother. I don't remember crying for my father, I screamed. I didn't cry for him until I was twelve. I suppose that is because I never understood the true meaning of his loss until then.

DEATH OF A BROTHER, SISTER, OR OTHER CLOSE RELATIVE

You're hit doubly hard when a sibling dies. First, because you lose someone who's a close member of your family. Second, the loss strikes so close to you that it's hard not to feel vulnerable

Young people aren't supposed to die. . . . How, then, could this happen?"
—Earl A. Grollman, American grief expert and rabbi[4]

yourself. In addition, the death of a child is a terrible loss to your parents, who will be deeply bereaved and disoriented by their loss. The ripple effects on most teenagers is severe.

If you lose an uncle, an aunt, a cousin, or some other relative, the situation is more unpredictable. The effects on you depend on how close you were to the person who died. In some families, though, these losses can hit as hard as a sibling's death.

Louisa, College Age

My brother was twenty-four when he was killed. . . . He had just gotten out of the hospital from getting his appendix out on the Friday morning, was told to go home and do nothing for a week. Just as he arrived here, his friend's father called him, said that this guy (I won't use names) was trying to kill himself, that he needed someone to sit with him till they could get some help. My brother said yes (he would never not help a friend in need). We went around there at six that night to pick him up, there was no one there, we looked in windows and saw nothing, so we went home. We were all ready for bed about ten or eleven that night, when his girlfriend and my other brother came running in, said he was in the hospital, that he had O.D.'d and it didn't look good. His girlfriend found them both on the floor, had to break in and call the hospital.

We all rushed to the hospital where he was on life support, he had stopped breathing for over thirty minutes and was most likely brain-dead. We turned the life support off at eleven A.M. on Sunday.

We learnt that the guy that he was trying to help had been going around (he was in a mental hospital for a few days) saying he was going to kill himself—and take someone with him. He had tried to kill his father the day before but no one told us about it. My brother was meant to go to Sydney [Australia] for an interview and health test to join the army, his only life dream, on the day we buried him. There would be no way on this earth that he would have used drugs. The only thing we have come up with is that my brother was in

> "Grief-stricken." Stricken is right; it is as though you had been felled. Knocked to the ground; pitched out of life and into something else.
> —Penelope Lively, English writer[5]

so much pain from his operation that he fell asleep/passed out and this guy injected him with heroin.

The police have told us that they know this guy did it, but there is no proof. . . . Therefore, he got away with it.

Sarah, Age Fifteen

My sister Bella died from injuries from a jeep accident. She was eighteen. The jeep flipped and she had her seat belt on—she broke her neck and her sternum was crushed. She would have graduated from high school five days later . . . and she was five months pregnant.

The night before, I attended an eighth-grade graduation party and spent the night with a friend. Technically it was my dad's weekend, but he was out of town at a tent sale for cars. Early Sunday morning (around six A.M.) the phone rang at my friend's house. I sat straight up and said, "That's my step-mom on the phone." Believe it or not, it was and she told me that Bella had been in a serious jeep accident and she didn't know where my mom was. I hurriedly woke up my friend's mother and we rushed to the hospital. There, I met my stepmother and gave as much information about Bella as I could to the hospital. I had also called my mother at her boyfriend's house and had to tell her about Bella's accident. My father was on his way from Montgomery and the rest of my family began to gather at the hospital. My mom came and for some reason, I wanted nothing to do with her. I remember going to the chapel and praying and hugging and crying with my stepmother. Somewhere around nine A.M. Bella died. Our priest came and so did the principal of my school. I met my dad out in the parking lot and broke the news to him. It was horrible.

Later that day, I accompanied my parents to the cemetery and helped choose the plot and then to the funeral home, where I met with the priest to plan her funeral. Both parents were great about involving me.

On Monday, I went to school, because that's what I was supposed to do. Everyone at school made me feel so weird that I called home and left. We had the wake that night and really wakes are not good—I ended up comforting more people rather

than the opposite. The casket was closed because she was so swollen. I saw her and later had many nightmares, yet I have no regrets for looking. The funeral was the next day and everyone came, including my class, in their school uniforms. She had eight priests there for her. That same afternoon, we went back to the same church for my eighth-grade graduation ceremony— I received a standing ovation for my diploma.

Zach, Mid-Teens

When I was thirteen, my mother gave birth to a baby boy who was premature, and a few hours later the baby died. I never even saw him. So in a way he wasn't really my brother—he wasn't anyone I felt I knew or had any kind of relationship with. But I still felt sad about what happened. Both of my parents seemed depressed when they lost the baby, and my mother cried off and on for a long time afterwards. I felt bad about that but didn't know what to do, so mostly I didn't say anything or do anything. But my little brother was still someone I thought about and wondered about. Even now that I'm older I still think about him now and then—what he would have been like, what we would have done together, things like that.

DEATH OF A GRANDPARENT

Many teens are close to their grandmothers and grandfathers. Some are dependent on grandparents for their day-to-day well-being as well as for emotional support. Depending on your cultural background, your grandparents may be as important a part of your family life as your parents and siblings; in other families, grandparents are more distant relatives—emotionally significant but not present for day-to-day activities. However, the death of a grandmother or grandfather is often a major event in a teenager's life.

> The death of a grandparent may be the first time that you are confronting death and witnessing the grief of those closest to you.
> —Earl A. Grollman, American grief expert and rabbi[6]

Evan, Late Teens at the Time of His Loss

When I was a senior in high school my mother's mother developed cancer—bowel cancer—and got very sick in just a few weeks. She lived in Wisconsin at the time. My mother and her younger sister flew there to take care of Grandma. I can't remember how long they stayed with her, but it wasn't very long because the cancer spread so fast. Mostly they were just trying to keep her comfortable and give her some company while she died.

Then at some point my mother called and asked if I wanted to come out and see Grandma while I had the chance. I said yes and took a plane to Wisconsin for a short visit. I wasn't eager to do that. Not because I didn't love her, 'cause I did, but I felt scared to have a conversation I knew would be real hard. I'd never been around someone who was dying before. I kind of imagined this gloomy scene of everyone sitting around the bed and crying. Also, I hadn't spent much time around my grandma for many years, so I didn't know what I'd say to her. So when I got there, I felt really uncomfortable and not sure what to do.

What actually happened was much different than what I

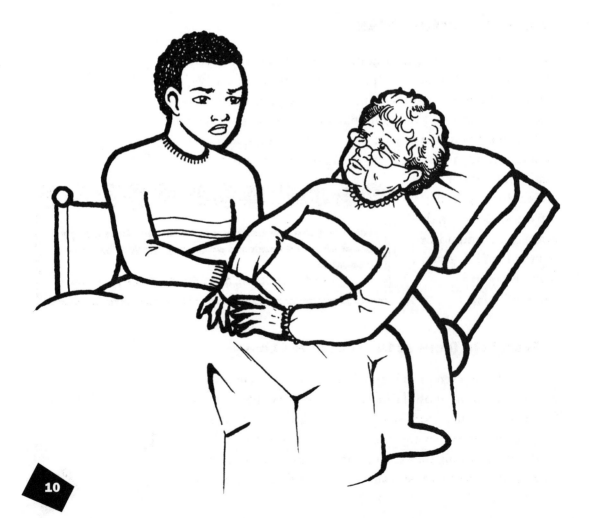

expected. My grandmother was very calm and not upset at all. She was fairly comfortable because of pain medications. Mostly she just sat in her bed and watched TV. She was this tiny little Italian-American woman, maybe four feet ten, wearing a cotton nightie and propped up on pillows. When I first got there, I felt so confused that I burst into tears, and she just hugged me and consoled *me*—as if *I* was the one who was suffering! She didn't seem at all upset. She just smiled and patted me on the shoulder and in her sing-songy accent said, "Sorry, sorry, I have no more tears, no more tears."

Theodore, Mid-Teens

My paternal grandfather died when I was sixteen. I'd never been close to him. He was very old even when I was a little kid, and as a teenager I found him creepy and I couldn't really talk with him about anything. Grandpa Ben was almost totally deaf, he had this strange huge hearing aid that didn't work very well, and he spent most of his time sitting in a huge leather chair and reading the newspaper. I tried to be nice to him, but we didn't have anything to talk about, and I found him frustrating because he seemed so senile. Then he had a series of strokes, ended up in a nursing home, and died.

I really didn't feel any particular sadness or loss when my dad told me that his father was dead. But I felt sorry for my dad. He didn't get upset—he just told us the news and said he felt relieved, since his father was so old and had so many health problems. They hadn't been very close, and since we lived so far away from Grandpa Ben my dad didn't see him very much, either. Then at dinner that night he started telling stories about his father—about his work as a surgeon, about what he'd been like as a family man, about how he'd been a lot more interesting than you could ever guess from knowing Grandpa Ben in his old age. He went on and on. I got restless and asked to be excused.

Later on I felt bad about that. I guess I felt uncomfortable. My dad wasn't the sort of guy who would break down and cry, and he didn't do anything like that at the time, so I figured he was all right about the whole thing. But he was upset in his own way, and I guess I should have been more thoughtful about what he was going through.

Janice, Mid-Teens

When my grandmother passed away I don't think I was mentally able to cope. [Janice's father had died several years earlier, and her grandmother's death stirred up a lot of feelings about the earlier loss.] I don't think I am ready to yet—publicly, anyway. I was scared to let people see me cry. I suppose it is okay to hide your feelings to the public, but it never did anyone any good to hide them permanently. Shortly before my grandmother was hospitalized I received a laptop to help me with schoolwork. That's when I truly began to cope with my father's death. I typed how I felt. I used writing as an outlet. I began to write even more after my grandmother died. It is my way to truly understand my feelings.

DEATH OF A FRIEND

The death of a friend hits teenagers hard in several ways. It's a terrible experience because you lose someone you care for—someone you *chose* to like, and to share your thoughts, feelings, and good times with. It's also a tough experience because it hits so close to home. When you're young, death seems so far away. Dying happens to old people, right? So it's an awful shock when someone who's as young as you ends up dying.

Everyone expects you to mourn for family members. But when a friend dies, teenagers are often left alone to deal with the pain.

—Earl A. Grollman, American grief expert and rabbi[7]

Jack, Late Teens

My best friend from about tenth grade on was a guy named Craig. He actually went to a different high school, but I met him through a mutual friend, and we hit it off from the start. I don't think I've ever gotten to be friends with someone so fast. Even the first time we met, we talked all day, went out to dinner at a local pizza place, then talked all evening till we had to quit. From then on we did all kinds of stuff together—went on double dates with our girlfriends, went hiking in the mountains, went to movies, goofed off, and hung out at each other's homes. You could say we were almost inseparable. Some people hassled us and said we were gay, but we weren't. We were just incredibly good friends.

I knew from the first few days of our friendship that Craig was a really troubled guy. He was brilliant and full of life. I don't think I've ever known anyone who lived each day so fully. But he had a gloomy side too, and he could get very depressed. He'd get into these very black moods and nothing could pull him out. He'd quote Winston Churchill about what he called "the Black Dog," which was his nickname for his depressions. He'd even joke about death: "I can't imagine I'll live long enough to go to college." Sometimes he'd do dangerous things that sort of flirted with death, like one time when we were driving on a mountain road at night, and suddenly he switched off the headlights, so we kept going along the road in pitch-black darkness. Craig scared me in some ways. He was so intense about everything! He never did anything halfway. Everything he did, he did full blast.

As I got to know him better, I learned about his home life, which was terrible—he had a terrible relationship with his parents, who were cold and judgmental toward him—and he told me at some point that he'd been in and out of a mental hospital for psychiatric problems. He even got hospitalized at one point our senior year. The hospital was called Mount Aerie. Craig hated the place but admitted that he felt better after spending a couple of weeks there than he'd felt before he went in. He also felt amused by some words he found on the invoice for his hospital bill. Just like at a hotel it said, "We Hope You Enjoyed Your Stay—Come Again!"

> To mourn is to be extraordinarily vulnerable. It is to be at the mercy of inside feelings and outside events in a way most of us have not been since early childhood.
> —Christian McEwen, English poet and writer[8]

One afternoon late in our senior year, Craig's girlfriend, Cathy, came to my house. I saw her pretty often but only with Craig, so I felt surprised to see her. I said, "What's up?" or something, but right away she said, "Craig's gone and killed himself." I assumed it was a joke—he was always doing crazy stuff and joking about suicide—so I said, "What? Again?" And Cathy said, "No, I mean it. He jumped off the Security Life building." That was the tallest building in town.

And it turned out to be true. He'd gone up there, climbed over the railing of the observation deck, and jumped.

I didn't know what to feel. I'd never lost a close friend before. In fact, nobody I'd known had died except maybe some really old relatives. Now Craig was dead. My best friend was dead. And he'd *chosen* to die. I felt awful. I knew he had all kinds of problems, and I knew about his hospitalizations, but I still couldn't help wondering if I could have done something to help him. Or maybe I'd made the situation worse by *not* doing something. Even if he got along so badly with his parents, maybe his friends could've made a difference. I don't know. . . .

DEATH OF A PET

Some people speak about a pet's death by using the word "only." "It's *only* a dog. . . ." "It's *only* a cat. . . ." But because

> Animals are such agreeable friends—they ask no questions, they pass no criticisms.[9]
> —George Eliot, English writer[10]

many teenagers, just like children and adults, have close relationships with animals, the death of a pet can strike with great force. A pet's death deprives you of a special companion, one you may have known and loved as long as the members of your family.

Annette, Age Sixteen

My sweet cat Luke is gone and I miss him so. My house is cold and empty without him. I wish I could make this feeling go away, I feel so hopeless and helpless knowing that he'll never be in my arms again. He'll never look at me with all the love in his eyes.

Tami, Age Eighteen

Last month we had to put my five-year-old Yorkie to sleep. She was a Christmas present when I was twelve. She fought so hard to stay with me these last four months, much to her vet's amazement. I'm having such a difficult time and I miss her so much it feels my heart is physically breaking. I don't know how to go on right now and I don't see a way out of this heartache. Sure, everyone says, "hang in there" or "it'll get better" but my question is *how?*

Alan, Age Nineteen

Last night me and my family got home from church to find my chocolate poodle, Harley, under my desk tangled in cords and her neck covered in blood. At first we couldn't find the source of the bleeding. It ended up being our other dog, a black lab, who'd caused the problem—we found a puncture wound on Harley's throat. It was too late. Harley had already lost too much blood. She was obviously in shock. We made her comfortable . . . covered her and kept her warm . . . talked to her . . . petted her . . . and waited. She finally died just after two A.M.

Our black lab, Raven is almost seven and 100 pounds and doesn't have an aggressive bone in her body. Raven is very

traumatized about what happened. I don't know what provoked her . . . what happened . . . or why. There has never been a problem between them. We found a ripped-open bag of Cheet-ohs in the middle of the floor. . . . My only guess is that Raven got them down and they fought over the Cheet-ohs. It was a long hard night with a lot of tears. We dropped Harley off at my vet the next day to be cremated and picked up her ashes about a week later. She will be missed.

Lesa, Age Fifteen

My cat Zoe passed away last month. I miss her! She died in the living room. I wrapped her in her blanket and my dad carried her to our new house that we are building and we placed her under the Christmas tree that we put up. She spent the rest of the night there. The next day we buried her in our yard beside my horse Jimmy. It was so hard to say good-bye to her.

> Animals were once, for all of us, teachers. They instructed us in ways of being and perceiving that extended our imaginations.
> —Joan McIntyre, American writer[11]

Marco, Age Seventeen

My dog, a three-year-old boxer, was killed around one A.M. on New Year's Eve by a car. It's only been two weeks but the pain is progressively getting worse. I feel like one of my parents has been taken from me. This is the first dog that I have ever had and the most special creature to ever enter my life. I wasn't expecting this to be so painful.

GRIEF—A BEGINNING, NOT THE END

These losses are significant, powerful, and painful. Most teenagers struggle with intense feelings of loss and grief. If you've experienced a similar loss, you probably feel confused, troubled, and hurt by what has happened. You may even feel paralyzed by sadness and fear following your loss. It's easy to imagine that you'll never feel better again.

But you will feel better. You'll adjust to your loss, make sense of what has happened, and move on into the rest of your life. Grief is a difficult task to face, but you'll deal with it creatively, as almost everyone does.

The first step is to understand grief and how it affects you.

NOTES

All names and some identifying characteristics (such as ages and city of residence) have been changed to protect the privacy of teenagers who have shared their stories with me.

1. Earl Grollman, *Straight Talk about Death for Teenagers: How to Cope with Losing Someone You Love* (Boston: Beacon, 1993), 43.

2. E. E. Wilkie, quoted in Beverley Raphael, *The Anatomy of Bereavement* (New York: Basic Books, 1983), 102.

3. See *The Quotations Page,* www.quotationspage.com.

4. Grollman, *Straight Talk about Death for Teenagers,* 49.

5. See *The Quotations Page,* www.quotationspage.com.
6. Grollman, *Straight Talk about Death for Teenagers,* 41.
7. Grollman, *Straight Talk about Death for Teenagers,* 54.
8. See *The Quotations Page,* www.quotationspage.com.
9. See *The Quotations Page,* www.quotationspage.com.
10. See *The Quotations Page,* www.quotationspage.com.
11. See *The Quotations Page,* www.quotationspage.com.

The Nature of Grief and Bereavement

I'd be the first person to say that the stories in chapter 1 are tough to read. Even so, I believe that it's important to think about the situations reflected in these stories. Why? Because they tell us a lot about loss and grief.

Each loss is different from every other loss, and what each person feels is unique to his or her own personality and experiences. Yet the events and feelings described here fall into certain patterns. Understanding those patterns can help you make sense of what you're feeling. What sorts of patterns? Well, patterns of intense and sometimes contradictory

> I felt lost. Bella was my only full-blooded sibling and we were close. I felt cheated. I wondered who would be my maid of honor when I got married. I was saddened by the fact that we wouldn't grow old together and our children wouldn't grow up together. I felt as if our whole family dynamics shifted, and the weight of being the oldest was tremendous. I felt very alone in my grief. . . . My friends did not know what to think. I just wanted to be normal and begin high school without this large amount of baggage. People look at you differently when you tell them your sister died.
>
> —Sarah, fifteen

emotions—patterns of difficult adjustment to the new "reality" following the loss—patterns of changes in how you perceive yourself and others. Grief may be unique to each individual, but it's a fundamental human experience. If you can understand that experience, you'll have an easier time dealing with it.

WHAT ARE GRIEF AND BEREAVEMENT?

"Bereavement is the reaction to the loss of a close relationship," according to Beverley Raphael, an Australian psychiatrist writing in *The Anatomy of Bereavement*.[1] Dr. Raphael and other experts believe that this reaction is one that human beings undergo to help them adapt to loss. If two people have a significant relationship and one of these persons dies, the survivor usually experiences some form of bereavement. The more significant the relationship, the more likely it is that bereavement will be intense. Bereavement is in some respects the cost of emotional commitment.

Although bereavement is a reaction, what follows it is a *process*. This process involves a variety of emotions (including sadness, longing, and bewilderment) that are collectively referred to as "grief"; the process includes social expressions, generally called "mourning." Bereavement, grief, and mourning are potentially confusing concepts. (Throughout this book, I use the terms *bereavement* and *grief* more or less interchangeably.) What is most important to remember is that these experiences are all part of a process. When someone you love has died, adjusting to the loss takes a while. The grief process doesn't happen all at once. It occurs over a period of time, often a longer time than you may find comfortable. It can't be rushed or compressed. But the grief process, though painful in many ways, has its own internal logic; if allowed to proceed, it almost always resolves successfully.

Here are two aspects of this situation to consider:

- First, bereavement and grief are normal experiences.
- Second, bereavement and grief are individual, highly personal experiences.

The Normality of Bereavement and Grief

For centuries, some people have tended to regard grief as a kind of illness. Even now you may hear of someone being "sick with grief." It's easy to understand why people might use this sort of expression. As Colin Murray Parkes and Robert S. Weiss have noted in their book *Recovery from Bereavement,* "After all, grief is a very painful condition that impairs the ability of the afflicted individual to function effectively in everyday activities. It produces a range of [bodily] symptoms: heaviness in the limbs, sighing, restless apathy, loss of appetite and weight, sleeplessness and languor, with pangs of acute distress."[2]

> There are . . . grounds for regarding grief as the "normal" accompaniment of a major loss. We see grief as a normal reaction to overwhelming loss, albeit a reaction in which normal functioning no longer holds.
> —Colin Murray Parkes, English psychiatrist, and Robert S. Weiss, American sociologist[3]

But these perceptions of grief as an illness ignore an important part of what happens during the grief process. A good comparison might be your body's response to a broken leg. The trauma to the bone is clearly harmful. You are in pain. If you ignore the injury or expect it to heal overnight, you may do yourself much worse damage than what you have already suffered. But if you let your body's capacity for self-healing do its work, you will recover. The broken bone may even end up stronger than it was before breaking.

The grief process is more complicated than the healing of broken bones, of course, and it's a subtler process as well. However, the basic analogy is appropriate. Bereavement is a human being's adjustment to major loss. This adjustment, as well as the grief you feel as part of it, is a sign of health, not a sign of its absence. Bereavement and grief are normal.

The Individualness of Bereavement and Grief

The grief process is also highly individual. Your experience won't necessarily resemble what anyone else goes through. After all, your relationship with the person you loved was unique; when he or she dies, your sense of loss too will be unique. Your personal background partially accounts for the individuality of what you feel when you suffer a loss. As Anne Rosberger, a therapist at the Bereavement and Loss Center in New York City, puts it, "Everybody comes into the situation of bereavement bringing with them a whole history. It's not as if they just came to this point and it's all entirely new. Every time you have a loss of any kind, other feelings around separation begin to surface. So you are bringing with it a lot of your past experience."[4]

For this reason, try to remember that you don't owe anyone any particular emotion, expression, set of words, or gestures during the course of your grief process. If people around you imply that you seem insufficiently grief stricken—perhaps you're not crying "enough"—then their reaction has more to do with their own expectations than with your feelings. The same holds true if you hear the message that you're too emotional, too upset, or too sad—likewise if anyone suggests that you are too giddy, too spacey, too nostalgic.

According to Marty Tousley, a bereavement counselor with Hospice of the Valley in Phoenix, Arizona, how teens react to a death depends on:

- How they've responded to other crises in their lives
- What was lost when this death happened (not only the life of the person who died, but certain aspects of the teen's own life as well)
- Who they were in their relationship with that person, and who they planned to be
- Their hopes and dreams for the future
- Who died (parent, sibling, grandparent, relative, friend, or some other person)
- How they lived together and what that person meant to them
- The person's role in their family
- When the death occurred (at what point in the life cycle: the teen's as well as that of the person who died)
- The circumstances surrounding the death, and how the death occurred. Family influences are important as well: size, solvency structure, style of coping, support and communication.[5]

In short, the nature of your experience depends on all the various factors that make any major life experience so individual.

23

No one can decide what your loved one meant to you; nor can anyone dictate the significance of that person's death. Wendy Foster-Evans, former bereavement coordinator, Hospice of Marin, San Rafael, California, describes the situation in these words: "People need to go through the grief process at their own pace and in their own way. Some people are very private about grief; others are really expressive. Either way, that's to be honored."[6]

BEREAVEMENT, GRIEF, AND EMOTIONS

The grief process usually includes intense emotions. The particular emotions, their intensity, and their duration vary from one person to another. Likely as not, however, you will experience some sort of grief—some sort of emotional reaction to the death and its consequences. These feelings are often surprising—either stronger, weaker, or different from what you might have expected. Marty Tousley describes this situation: "How loss, grief and mourning are experienced and expressed will vary among teens, just as it varies among all individuals. Everyone grieves differently, according to their age, gender, personality, culture, value system, understanding of death, past experience with loss and available support (from the teen's own family as well as support from peers and others outside the family). Grieving differs among members of the same family, as each person's relationship with and attachment to the deceased family member varies."[7]

Here are some of the typical emotional reactions during bereavement:

Shock

One of the most common emotions right after a loss is shock. This emotion is especially common if the death occurs without warning, but you may feel a sense of shock even if someone you love has died after a long illness. No matter how aware you may have been in advance, you're never entirely prepared for the death of someone you love.

> When Dad died I just couldn't believe it. He wasn't that old—just in his fifties—and he never, ever got sick. But then he got sick anyway and died practically overnight. I felt like somebody dropped a piano on me. For weeks after that I felt dazed and confused and really out of it.
>
> —Jason, late teens
>
> I felt crushed, shocked, shattered.
>
> —Michelle, thirteen

Beverley Raphael states that during a state of shock, "The bereaved person feels a sense of unreality, as though . . . it must be happening to someone else. The bereaved may feel distance from the horror and its implications, frozen in time. There is a feeling of being in a dream or a nightmare from which he will awake."[8] You may find it hard to believe that someone could be so fully present at one moment and totally gone the next. The death of someone you love seems a strange, incomprehensible disappearing act.

Shock is generally an emotion that fades within a few days or weeks. Yet at times it can be remarkably durable. If your loved one has died in an accident or from an unexpected, sudden illness, you may find it difficult to believe that the death has occurred at all. You may find yourself mistaking a stranger's voice for that of the person you knew, or you may catch sight of someone you imagine to be that person. These perceptual tricks are disturbing. You may worry that you're hallucinating or even going crazy. The writer Anne Morrow Lindbergh eloquently describes this state of mind: "One must go through periods of numbness that are harder to bear than grief."[9] However, many people experience these tricks of the mind. They are merely side effects of shock and almost always harmless. Once your mind has had a while to adjust to a sudden and confusing change, the sense of shock and its effects will diminish.

Sadness and Depression

When someone you love has died, you will probably experience sadness, depression, or both. The difference between these two reactions is important but often not recognized in our era. Both reactions are common expressions of bereavement.

John Bowlby, an English psychiatrist whose studies of bereavement and grief form the basis of much research on the subject, states in his book *Loss,* one of the fundamental books on the subject, that "sadness is a normal and healthy response to any misfortune. Most, if not all, more intense episodes of sadness are elicited by the loss, or expected loss, either of a loved person or else of family."[10] Sadness during the grief process is essentially an emotional response to the finitude of human life. It is a recognition that something important is over; someone important to you is gone.

By contrast, Dr. Bowlby regards depression as a condition that is "an inevitable accompaniment of any state in which behavior becomes disorganized, as it is likely to do after a loss." Depression is a way in which your mind distances itself from disruptive changes in your life and allows you time to reorganize. Depression, however, often seems less an emotion than an *absence* of emotion. It frequently resembles a kind of fatigue, a sense of emptiness or disconnection from the world.

What is most important to remember about both sadness and depression is that not only are they normal but they almost always diminish with the passage of time. Sadness and depression are parts of the complicated adjustment to loss that

I felt very sad. The most difficult thing for me to deal with was that Grampa had to go in the cold hard ground.

—Janie, sixteen

you are making. Although many people feel acutely sad or depressed following someone's death, few end up being overwhelmed by their emotions. Almost all bereaved persons find that their sadness and depression let up after a while and that the pain they feel gradually gives way to more comfortable emotions. (If you find that depression continues for more than a few weeks, however, or if it impairs your daily activities, you should seek help. We'll discuss this issue in chapter 7.)

Relief

A sense of relief may cause feelings of worry or embarrassment in many people following a loss. How can you feel relieved that someone you love has died? Our culture prompts you to feel that relief following someone's death is inappropriate. But relief, like other emotions, is often a normal response to a loss. Why shouldn't you feel relieved in some situations, such as when a severely ill person's suffering has ended? Shock, sadness, and other emotions complicate a sense of relief, but they don't contradict it.

After a loved one's long illness, most relatives feel relieved that the suffering is over. You may end up feeling a similar kind of relief—perhaps relief that you are now spared further effort, emotional upheaval, or family conflict. These are understandable emotions.

Relief sometimes follows a death not just because the illness is over but also because the person is now gone. If you had a conflicted relationship, for instance—especially if the person who died had been abusive toward you—it would not be at all surprising if you feel relieved. Yet even if you felt close to the deceased person, you may experience relief that the complexities of getting along are now over.

There's nothing wrong with a sense of relief under these circumstances. Although everyone wishes that relationships could be happy and supportive, reality often falls short of these expectations. Relief following the end of a difficult relationship is certainly appropriate. Even relief following a good relationship isn't unusual, surprising, or bad.

Mom fought against cancer for almost five years. First she had breast cancer. Then she developed other kinds of cancer when the breast tumors spread. She was sick during almost all of my teenage years. When she died I felt terrible—really depressed and angry—but I also felt relieved because all her suffering was over. That was hard because I didn't think I had a right to feel relieved.

—Amanda, seventeen

My mom and I were very close. You could almost say we were *too* close—we were so alike, and I felt this constant need to do what she did and win her approval on everything. When she died I felt terrible, and I still miss her, and she was definitely the person I've been closest to all along. But you know what? After a while I realized that I have some independence now that I never had before, and I can do things now that I would never have considered before, just because Mom wouldn't have done them that way.

—Nina, nineteen

I felt terrible when my friend Leo died but I guess I felt relief, too, 'cause I know I could've been in an accident just like him, but I wasn't. I felt bad about that [feeling relief] but everybody told me there was nothing I could do. You can't feel bad about not having such a terrible thing happen to you.

—Jared, late teens

Regret and Guilt

Perhaps you feel that you should have done more for the person you loved. You should have done things differently. You should have said more, said less, said something other than what you ended up saying. Well, those feelings too are common and normal. After someone's death, any mistakes and errors of judgment made during the relationship can make you feel that you failed or fell short in some respects. According to Dr. Raphael's *The Anatomy of Bereavement,* "Regret over what has been lost, what cannot be achieved now without the dead person, are . . . common emotions." In addition: "Guilt is frequent: it relates to the imperfection of human relationships."[11]

However, even a more satisfying relationship can produce regrets. The demands of caring for a sick relative, for instance, are a potential source for guilt. Few people emerge from the ordeal unscathed. Julie Walker and Marcia Lattanzi, both bereavement counselors at Boulder County Hospice in Colorado, summarize the situation in this manner: "Guilt is a very prominent emotion in bereavement. It is usually expressed in the desire to have *done more* or to have *said* something to the deceased while he or she was still living. In simple terms, it is a punishment of the self for seemingly not living up to one's expectations of him/herself."[12] Kim Smith, a grief counselor at the Fellow Traveller, a provider of support services and online counseling in England, puts it this way: "Guilt [is] common for teens. Examples: wishing people dead who then go on to die. . . . The parent dies after scolding a teen but before the trouble has passed. . . . Unfinished business. . . . Relating misbehavior as contributory factor to death ('If I hadn't upset him he wouldn't have been driving so fast')."[13] In short, guilt is a common reaction during the grief process.

> I kept thinking, "Maybe I could've done something different." I was just the little sister, not the parent, but I couldn't help wondering. I don't know. . . . It's like when my sister died I felt responsible even though I knew I wasn't.
>
> —Sarah, fifteen

But it's important to keep these issues in context. First, the *presence* of guilt doesn't mean that you have *reason* to feel guilty. Guilt may simply be a side effect of ordinary human fallibility. It seems almost impossible to love someone and *not* end up feeling guilty when he or she endures a harsh illness or a sudden death. You wanted to make a difference, but you couldn't—or at least you couldn't to the degree that you would have liked. For this reason, the guilt and regret are common experiences. These feelings may be subtle or intense, but they are there. But as Virginia A. Simpson, executive director of the Mourning Star Center (a grief counseling organization in California) says, "First of all, teens . . . need to know that it is not their fault. The loss [they have experienced] is not because they were bad or are being punished by God."[14]

Second, keep in mind that the grief process intensifies most feelings. As a consequence of your grief, you may be recalling missed opportunities and errors of judgment in ways that distort their real importance within your relationship. This isn't to say that shortcomings didn't exist or that mistakes didn't occur; however, they may not have been as significant as you imagine.

Anger

Like guilt, anger is common following bereavement—though you may regard anger, like relief, as a "forbidden" emotion. How can you be angry at someone who died? How can you be angry at someone *for* dying? Sadness may seem appropriate in your mind, but anger doesn't. Yet as Dr. Bowlby and other researchers

have noted, many people—if not most—feel some sort of anger in the aftermath of a relative's death: anger at being abandoned, anger at being left with bills to pay or problems to solve, anger at having expended so much effort in an ultimately hopeless cause.

These are all understandable reactions. Anger may not be pretty or comfortable, but it often makes sense. Your loved one's death has put you under stress. It may have demanded your time, attention, patience, or self-denial. It has ultimately deprived you of someone of great significance in your life. Why shouldn't you be angry? What makes

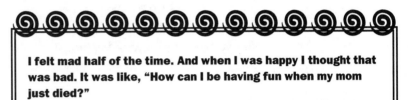

> I felt mad half of the time. And when I was happy I thought that was bad. It was like, "How can I be having fun when my mom just died?"
>
> —Sarah, fifteen

anger difficult is that it's often socially unacceptable to express what you feel toward the people or institutions you hold responsible—doctors, nurses, hospitals, and so forth. Or else the object of your wrath is beyond your reach—fate, God, or the universe. Perhaps the most difficult situation is anger toward someone you love. Feeling angry at someone who has died usually seems awkward, unfair, ungrateful.

Yet in some respects, all these kinds of anger are appropriate. Medical personnel and institutions make mistakes. Fate turns out to be unfair. Anger is a predictable reaction to all these developments. There's no reason to feel embarrassed or frightened by your anger. It is, however, important to express it appropriately. Sometimes a counselor or therapist can be useful in sorting out different kinds of anger and anticipating their effects on your life.

> I felt angry at everyone. At Mom for dying, at the doctors for letting her die, at my family for being so messed up afterwards, at the minister for saying the same old stuff at the funeral, at everyone for everything. And at myself for feeling so helpless and miserable.
>
> —Rachel, sixteen

Longing

You may find that you can accept your loved one's death a short time after it occurs. However, you may also find that the loss produces intense and sometimes protracted longing for that person. Like other emotions that surface during the bereavement process, longing can cause you to worry that something is amiss. But also like the other emotions, longing is a normal reaction to loss.

Perhaps you feel that longing is inappropriate. You feel you should be mature and independent. You may therefore feel that longing implies neediness. In fact, you can be fully functioning—you may have helped the person you loved in many ways—and still feel a sense of longing. Longing isn't necessarily a sign of emotional reliance. Instead, longing simply indicates how deep your bond was. It's an acknowledgment of how strong a relationship can grow when people truly care for one another.

> For a long time after Craig died, I missed him more than I could tell anybody. We were really, really close friends. . . . But I didn't say anything about missing him, 'cause some people would misunderstand.
>
> —Jack, late teens

THE PHASES OF THE GRIEF PROCESS

Which of these emotions you feel, when, and to what degree will depend on many circumstances. Some of these circumstances are a result of bereavement in general—that is, a result of the effects that you would feel following *any* loss. Others are more specific to what follows the loss of someone with whom you had a special kind of relationship, such as a parent, a sibling, or a close friend. Still others are unique to your own personality.

However, now that we've examined them separately, it's worth noting that these emotions don't usually occur one by one but rather in combinations, and often in a fairly predictable sequence.

During the past several decades, thanatologists—the social scientists who study death and grief—have identified several phases that people go through during the grief process. These phases make it easier to understand what formerly seemed a shapeless, confusing jumble of experiences.

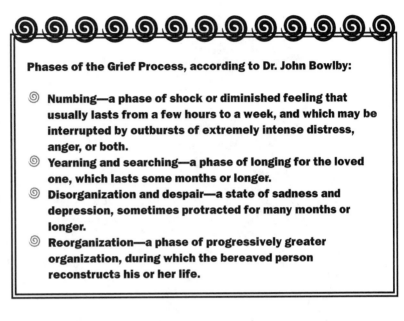

Phases of the Grief Process, according to Dr. John Bowlby:

- **Numbing**—a phase of shock or diminished feeling that usually lasts from a few hours to a week, and which may be interrupted by outbursts of extremely intense distress, anger, or both.
- **Yearning and searching**—a phase of longing for the loved one, which lasts some months or longer.
- **Disorganization and despair**—a state of sadness and depression, sometimes protracted for many months or longer.
- **Reorganization**—a phase of progressively greater organization, during which the bereaved person reconstructs his or her life.

The most persuasive theory of phases during the grief process is that formulated by Dr. John Bowlby, whom I've quoted earlier. Writing in *Loss,* Dr. Bowlby states that people go through four phases of grieving after the loss of a close relative. These phases are numbing; yearning and searching; disorganization and despair; and reorganization.

Most people experience all of these phases in one way or another. However, the grief process rarely proceeds in a smooth, even flow from one experience to another. Instead, it often involves a mixture of emotions—sometimes with considerable uncertainty and ambivalence along the way. As John Bowlby states, "Admittedly these phases are not clear-cut, and any one individual may oscillate [go back and forth] for a time between any two of them."[15]

In addition, the nature of your relationship and the circumstances of the other person's death make a difference in what you experience during these phases. A sudden loss will affect you differently from a loss that you've anticipated. The loss of a parent will affect you differently from the loss of a brother or sister, which in turn will affect you differently from the loss of a friend, and so forth. But overall, as Dr. Bowlby explained to me in an interview, "I think this general scheme is applicable toward almost all experiences of bereavement. It is either much intensified in certain situations, or very much modified and attenuated [diminished]. But this overall pattern applies to all forms of bereavement experiences."[16]

One other important consideration: these emotions are often closely interrelated. They can intensify and even trigger each other. For instance, if your loved one died after a long illness, your sadness over the long process of dying can heighten a sense of regret that you couldn't or didn't do more to help. Guilt can augment your anger that doctors and nurses weren't more supportive. Anger can in turn feed both sadness and guilt.

The interactions can go on and on. The particular pattern of emotions varies from one person to another, or even within one person from one time to another. Sometimes the interactions are difficult to follow, let alone understand. The important thing is to be aware that the jumble of emotions is almost inevitable—and that it will subside.

If you have heard that grief occurs in a fixed set of "stages," it's worth noting that social scientists have developed theories about the phases of the grief process as theoretical tools, not as precise ways of determining what any one person should or will feel following a loss. The grief process has a certain order to it, but it progresses through what are actually overlapping, fluid phases. You will cause yourself undue worry if you expect your thoughts and feelings to follow a straightforward course during the grief process. As the writer Mason Cooley puts it, "Like love, grief fades in and out."[17]

What teens say about the phases of the grief process:
For a long time I didn't let myself feel anything at all. Then it was everything at once. After a while things settled down.

—Marcia, seventeen

When I am alone at night, it is usually when it hits me. I cry and sometimes it really hurts but I think it is as important to cry as it is to laugh.

—Kerry, fifteen

Sometimes I didn't know what I was feeling.

—Jamal, seventeen

I thought it [intense grief] would never end, but eventually it did.

—Natalie, eighteen

Sometimes it [intense emotion] tickles your toes, other times it knocks you down.

—Louisa, late teens

DURATION OF THE GRIEF PROCESS

How long do these emotions last? This question is difficult to answer. The duration of intense emotions during the grief process varies enormously. Anne Rosberger at Bereavement and Loss Center in New York City states, "Most people want to know, 'How long am I going to feel this way?' When you're in pain, you want to know that there's an end point. You can tolerate a certain amount of anxiety and pain if you know that at such-and-such time, it'll all be over. I wish we had a crystal ball. But we don't. It really is so individually determined."[18]

The comments of the people I've interviewed show an enormous range of response. Some people feel strong emotions for only a few days or weeks. Others remain upset for months, even years. What you experience depends on your own personality, your state of physical and emotional health, your relationship with your loved one, the circumstances of the death, your social support system, and other factors. Precisely because the interaction of these variables makes for enormously varied responses, you should keep in mind that there is no single "right" sequence of events. Normal responses range from those in which people feel little or no distress to those in which people feel bereaved for several years.

> Everyone expects you to be over it in a month or so—they don't understand unless they have lost someone. I actually spent the beginning of this new year crying in a corner.
>
> —Louisa, late teens

What you can assume is that the intensity of your grief reaction—whatever your particular emotions—most often lets up gradually. Also, these emotions tend to be recurrent. As Dr. Ann York, a psychiatrist at the Child and Family Consultation Centre in London, England, says, "Symptoms of grief lessen in intensity over eighteen months or so. . . . Many adolescents report some symptoms for many years, as do adults."[19] But even when you feel you're "done"—when you expect to feel no more anger, sadness, or regret—the feelings can well up again. Such recurrences, like the slow subsiding of emotions, are also normal. Grief is rarely something that you can have "over and done with" and never feel again. Yet if you allow it to run its course, the grief process almost always resolves itself satisfactorily.

NOTES

1. Beverley Raphael, *The Anatomy of Bereavement* (New York: Basic Books, 1983), 24.

2. Colin Murray Parkes and Robert S. Weiss, *Recovery from Bereavement* (New York: Basic Books, 1983), 45.

3. Parkes and Weiss, *Recovery from Bereavement*, 47.

4. Anne Rosberger, private interview.

5. Marty Tousley, private e-mail correspondence.

6. Wendy Foster-Evans, private interview.

7. Marty Tousley, private e-mail correspondence.

8. Raphael, *The Anatomy of Bereavement*, 89.

9. See www.quotationspage.com.

10. John Bowlby, *Attachment and Loss,* vol. 3, *Loss* (New York: Basic Books), 1980.

11. Raphael, *The Anatomy of Bereavement,* 53.

12. Marcia Lattanzi, private interview.

13. Kim Smith, private e-mail correspondence.
14. Virginia A. Simpson, private e-mail correspondence.
15. Bowlby, *Loss,* 126.
16. Bowlby, private interview.
17. See www.quotationspage.com.
18. Anne Rosberger, private interview.
19. Ann York, private e-mail correspondence.

3 Kinds of Loss

As the previous chapter explains, grief isn't just one experience—it's a complex, highly individual cluster of emotions that takes place over a period of time. I urge you to accept the individuality of your own grief and allow yourself to feel your own emotions throughout the grief process. Chapters 5 and 6 will offer suggestions for how to come to terms with bereavement.

First, though, it's important to realize that bereavement following a sudden death (such as the result of an accident or sudden illness) differs from bereavement following a more prolonged process of dying (such as a long illness).

DEALING WITH SUDDEN DEATH

When someone you love dies suddenly, the loss can hit with great intensity. It seems impossible that someone you may have known for years—someone you may have seen that same day—is now gone forever. The resulting sense of shock can be a major part of your bereavement.

Here's why. The aftermath of a loved one's illness or accident forces a new reality on you without warning, but your sense of the world doesn't change so fast. "When death occurs with little or no warning," according to Beverley Raphael's *The Anatomy of Bereavement,* "there has been no opportunity for anticipation, for preparation beforehand. The death brings an extra effect of shock over and above the normal."[1] You probably find it hard to believe that the terrible event has really happened. You keep expecting the situation to change. This sense of denial is a normal part of bereavement, but it's generally most intense following a sudden death. For this reason, the first task facing you after a loved one's sudden death is one of the hardest—to accept the reality of your loss.

Let's examine these issues in a little more detail. Later in this chapter, we'll also explore how you feel when your loved one dies following a longer illness.

Denial and Disbelief following a Sudden Death

The sudden death of someone you love usually causes you to deny or doubt your loss. The English psychologist Colin Murray Parkes and the American sociologist Robert S. Weiss, writing in *Recovery from Bereavement,* regard denial as "a type of distancing produced by a refusal to acknowledge reality."[2] Disbelief is similar—though it's less a refusal than an *inability* to acknowledge what has happened. Either way, these reactions are almost universal during the early phases of bereavement. Disbelief is understandable in these situations.

> It didn't make sense. I flew back home expecting the usual scene, but instead I ended up waiting in the hospital and this doctor was saying my dad was dead. I felt this total sense of unreality.
> —**Michael, nineteen**

Denial and disbelief are important because they allow your mind to "buy time" while adjusting to a harsh and hurtful new reality. This state of mind is probably inevitable during the early days of bereavement. Don't let it alarm you; the sense of unreality will pass. When you're psychologically ready, you'll begin to accept the truth of your loss, and you'll deal with it at your own rate.

Reactions to Sudden and Not-Sudden Deaths

Bereavement experts have noted differences in how survivors react to sudden and not-sudden deaths. For instance, Beverley Raphael believes that if someone you love dies from a protracted illness, you "may go through a number of processes with phases of denial, angry protest, and sad acceptance"

before the death has even occurred. These processes can provide a kind of "head start" in bereavement.[3] By comparison, a loved one's sudden death deprives you of a chance to anticipate the death. You lack a chance to grieve in advance.

Yet as Dr. Raphael and other experts have noted, the differences between the two situations are more than just the potential for a head start. Parkes and Weiss found in their research that expected and unexpected losses often took different courses. People who learned of a loved one's unexpected death didn't necessarily *disbelieve* what they were told; rather, they weren't able to grasp its full implications. In contrast, people who had been warned of a forthcoming loss responded differently. They felt greater anxiety and tension on being told of the seriousness of the person's condition, and they sometimes tried to avoid accepting the facts of the situation. But this anticipatory reaction wasn't as severe as the reaction experienced by the unexpectedly bereaved. In short, the nature of bereavement itself seemed to differ in expected and unexpected losses.[4] The implication: whether a death is sudden or not sudden seems to be one of the most important considerations in determining how you respond to it.

Abrupt Changes in Circumstances

Following a loved one's death, teenagers often face changes in their personal circumstances—who will be supporting them, looking after them, living with them, and so forth. In the aftermath of a sudden death, you face these changes all at once. The nature of these changes may be similar following a sudden death and following anticipated deaths. However, sudden death can make the changes more difficult.

For instance, you may have to take on new responsibilities in the aftermath of a parent's death. The situation will depend on your age, your family circumstances, your surviving parent's financial situation, and other issues. What Michael faced following his father's death is a good example. Within a few days or weeks after that, he helped his mother deal with totally unfamiliar tasks: arranging a funeral, collecting insurance money, investing the funds in stocks and bonds, and deciding

whether to sell or keep the family house. Fortunately, Michael's mother was able to perform most of these legal and financial tasks. But Michael took on responsibilities he'd never imagined facing at the age of nineteen. He felt stressed by the situation yet able to handle it. The *suddenness* of having to deal with these issues, however, was a problem—more of a problem than the tasks themselves.

Denial and disbelief, reactions to sudden and not-sudden deaths, and abrupt changes in personal circumstances all affect you in the aftermath of a sudden death. Before we look at the effects in detail, however, let's explore another important issue.

Kinds of Sudden Death

In addition to the circumstances we've discussed, there is the question of what *kind* of death your loved one died. Whether the situation involved acute illness, an accident, suicide, or homicide makes a difference in how you face the aftermath and how you should deal with it.

Acute Illness

The most common cause of sudden death in adults is acute illness. Heart attacks and strokes kill many thousands of men and women each year, often without warning. In addition, other ailments kill thousands of other adults with only a few days' or weeks' warning.

"Because there is such an intense battle for life [during an acute illness]," Dr. Raphael states in *The Anatomy of Bereavement,* "the possibilities of death may be put aside in the fight for survival. Then the suddenness of the death, despite forewarning, still brings great shock, although perhaps not so much as in those deaths that are immediate."[5] In addition, some medical crises that are no longer considered routinely fatal (pneumonia, bowel obstructions, appendicitis, and so forth) sometimes result in death regardless of modern medicine.

Accidents

Many tens of thousands of Americans die in accidents each year. If your loved one dies in an accident, you may struggle with feelings that the death made no sense. Some illnesses lend themselves to fairly straightforward explanations—your father had had high blood pressure, your sister had developed a defective heart valve, and so forth. But accidents are often harder to rationalize. A drunk driver swerves into oncoming traffic; a construction crew lets some materials fall; a wire short-circuits— these and many other situations make it difficult to believe that the loss you've suffered really makes sense. This senselessness can make your grief more intense and more difficult.

> The thing I hated most about Leo's accident was that it was *so stupid!!!* It was just the most pointless thing, and that made his death much, much worse than it was already.
> —Jared, late teens

Another potential problem is that you may have been involved in the accident as well, which can affect your own bereavement. "If others are involved in the accident, the death may become a shared traumatic experience," writes Dr. Raphael. "You may be struggling to overcome your own injuries. You may also feel a complicated mix of relief and guilt because your loved one died but you yourself survived."[6] These are the main reasons why the aftermath of an accident can be so emotionally difficult.

Homicide and Suicide

The situation is still more complex if the death was a result of suicide or homicide. Under any circumstances, suicide is one of the most difficult kinds of loss to face. Disbelief, hurt, and anger are all normal emotions following the death of someone you love, and these feelings are even more intense in the aftermath of suicide. Similarly, the relatives and friends of someone who has been murdered feel shocked, outraged, and bewildered. Both of these situations present all the usual difficulties that follow a sudden death plus especially heavy burdens of anger or guilt.

In the aftermath of homicide, "the shock of the death is complicated by hate for the killer and preoccupation with judgment and retribution," according to Dr. Raphael. "The violence of these deaths compounds the trauma and shock effects of sudden death."[7]

In addition to the anger toward the murderer, you may well feel angry toward other people. Evelyn Gladu, former director of Omega, a bereavement counseling center in the Boston area, works with relatives of homicide victims. "What seems to be a big target of the anger is the whole judicial system," she stated in an interview. "The fumblings and red tape and all the time involved these days make people almost as angry as the actual perpetrator does."[8] Of course, legal proceedings after a homicide may provide the relatives with a needed sense of justice; yet the length and complexity of

> I hated those guys for killing my cousin but I hated everyone else, too. Even the people on "our side" made me furious because they were a constant reminder of what had happened.
> —LaRonda, eighteen

If you're grieving the death of someone you love in the aftermath of a homicide, according to John Nagel, MD, a psychiatrist in Fort Collins, Colorado, "your anger and outrage are *right there*. You're less likely to postpone anger and grief, which will be very immediate." In some respects this immediacy of feeling is good—you won't ignore or deny what you're feeling. But as Dr. Nagel goes on to say, "The risk for teenagers is that you may translate your anger into impulsive action, which can cause you more problems in the long run." You can't lash out indiscriminately. Instead, "you have to let the justice system do its work. But at the same time, you need to connect with someone who is compassionate, trustworthy, sincere, someone who ideally has some experience and wisdom regarding these things. For a teen, that person is *not* your peers, who have no experience with these things. Psychotherapy may be useful. Talking to your school counselor may be useful."[9]

these proceedings can be profoundly frustrating even if the criminal justice system succeeds in finding, trying, and punishing the killer.

Louisa, quoted in chapter 1, is a good example of this situation. Her brother Tad's friend, intent on committing homicide/suicide, had murdered Tad by injecting him with a lethal dose of heroin. In addition to having to face the loss of her brother, Louisa struggled with her anger at the senselessness of a disturbed youth's murderous act. Her family couldn't seek retribution through the court system, because the perpetrator was already dead.

We knew Craig was suicidal. He talked about it, joked about it, and did things that sort of bounced back and forth between just goofing around and being downright self-destructive. Sometimes he'd drive in unsafe ways. He'd walk in the street at night and almost get hit by cars. One time he went hiking in the mountains, got caught in a snowstorm, got lost, and nearly froze to death. All of us who knew him were aware that Craig was in bad shape. It wasn't really a question of if but when he'd try to kill himself. But we didn't know what to do. His parents knew he was suicidal, his teachers knew, the school counselors knew, his minister knew, and we knew. All we could do was try to be caring friends, talk to him, and hope he wouldn't do something really drastic.

"When he went ahead and jumped off that building, I couldn't stop thinking about what had happened, and I couldn't stop wondering if maybe I could have made a difference if I'd known what he was planning. A bunch of us went out to a movie the night before. Craig seemed restless—got up a lot during the movie and went back to the concession area—but that's just the way he was. I thought maybe he just needed the bathroom! The next morning, he killed himself. So I kept thinking: should I have known? Should I have maybe said something? You can't help wondering.

—Jack, late teens

Suicide also can be a profoundly difficult form of sudden death for survivors to cope with. The reason: suicide also evokes powerful feelings of rejection and hurt. As Aleta Koman, a psychotherapist in Arlington, Massachusetts, explains, "It's common for friends and family to feel 'survivor guilt' following a suicide. Everyone plays what I call the 'If Only' game—'if only I'd done this, if only I'd done that.' People have rescue fantasies and blame themselves because they couldn't save the person who died."[10] Suicide is most traumatic for the survivors because of its legacy of uncertainty, guilt, blame, and hostility.

The reality of the situation, however, is that no one—not you, not anyone else—can prevent the suicide of someone who's intent on dying. Psychologists still don't fully understand the causes of suicidal behavior. In many instances, biochemical imbalances are a contributing factor. In others, severe personal problems are the primary source. You can't take responsibility for your loved one's self-destructive actions. All you can do now is look after yourself, deal with your loss, and work through the process of your own bereavement.

As with the aftermath of homicide, what you face after a suicide may be something you shouldn't attempt to confront alone. It's

Here are some suggestions from Edwin Bokert, a psychologist and psychotherapist in northern New Jersey: "First of all, try to be aware of what you may be doing to block your feelings, or to avoid working on those feelings. Be aware of 'self-anesthesia.' That can lead to risky behaviors such as drug use, alcohol abuse, sexual acting out, and addictive behaviors such as binge eating. But you need to feel your own feelings, not ignore them. You can't drug 'em, drink 'em, or sex 'em away. Also, be aware of self-destructive behavior. If you seem accident-prone and distractible, or if you're neglecting your activities, friendships, or schoolwork, reach out to someone for help."[11]

true that you can probably work your way through some of the issues and feelings on your own terms. But if you feel you're really struggling with the aftermath of your loss, you may have an easier, less stressful time if you can find a thoughtful and supportive guide to help you figure things out and start to move on.

For specific resources in the aftermath of a friend's or family member's suicide, see the section called "Suicide Prevention and Counseling" in chapter 9, on resources.

After-Effects of Sudden Death

Following a loved one's sudden death, you may experience certain after-effects that can be confusing or upsetting.

Frozen Images

Sudden death can create a special burden during the grief process if the last moments you spent with someone you care for were hostile, angry, gruesome, or sad. Because of unfortunate timing, an otherwise happy or pleasant relationship can end up distorted or marred by the final image of conflict or suffering. An example of this situation is Jim, seventeen years old, who witnessed his father's fatal heart attack. In this and many other situations, a sudden death can leave a sense of uncertainty, distaste, or repugnance in its aftermath.

Coming to terms with the unknown or shocking circumstances may be a difficult task during the grief process. However, keep in mind that "final" images aren't as final as they seem. Many people experience a lingering of images of death or suffering, which can add to your grief, but even these images will eventually ease. In time, you'll find that the older, happier memories will return. Don't worry—you won't remember your loved one only as they were at the moment of death.

Unfinished Business

If someone you love dies suddenly, you may miss out on an opportunity to discuss concerns and worries, to resolve old conflicts, and to say good-bye. You may end up feeling that the relationship ended with a lot of "unfinished business."

Danielle was eighteen when her dad died of a brain aneurysm. Although many misunderstandings had existed between father and daughter, Danielle figured that they'd have a chance to "iron things out" eventually. They didn't; the father's death made that impossible. As a result, Danielle felt deprived of the opportunity she'd craved to have a less hostile, more accepting father–daughter relationship.

The issue of unfinished business is particularly upsetting because there's no simple solution to the problem. What you didn't do for your loved one can't be done now. What you didn't tell him or her can't be said now. Coming to terms with death and loss necessarily involve accepting these unfortunate realities. Yet accepting them doesn't mean that you can't come to terms with them. Chapters 5 and 6 suggest a variety of ways in which you can approach the issues of unfinished business.

Acceptance and Beyond

I wish I could say that there's an easy way to resolve these issues. The truth is, however, that grief following a loved one's sudden death can last for a long time. But rest assured that its power isn't absolute or permanent. Although the images and memories of your loved one's death may linger, they will diminish after a while. You'll eventually regain a sense of stability and continuity within your life. You'll gain a sense of the past and its place in your family. You'll develop a new sense of who your loved one was and of what he or she gave you during your time together.

Even a completely unexpected death can't overwhelm the reality of whatever was good in your relationship with the person who died. Gentler, happier recollections will return in time. Your capacities for emotional health are stronger than the stress of loss. Chapters 5 through 6 will suggest ways to explore and express those capacities.

DEALING WITH DEATH FOLLOWING A PROLONGED ILLNESS

A loved one's prolonged illness spares you some of the shock that follows a sudden death; it allows you more time to prepare emotionally for what's happening. This additional time—months, even years—can make bereavement easier in some respects. It can allow you a more gradual adjustment to loss and a chance to strengthen good relationships, repair bad ones, heal old wounds, and say good-bye.

Yet a long illness involves its own hardships. Your relative or friend may suffer from a painful and debilitating disease that causes you great anguish. He or she may undergo personality changes that strain your relationship. In some cases (such as a parent's illness) you may end up with family responsibilities that most teenagers don't have to carry. Also, of course, when your loved one dies after a long illness, the loss is similar in some respects to what you would experience following a sudden death. Your loved one is dead. The relationship is over. You must now deal with the loss and, in time, get on with life.

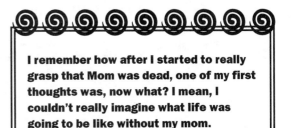

I remember how after I started to really grasp that Mom was dead, one of my first thoughts was, now what? I mean, I couldn't really imagine what life was going to be like without my mom.
—Arielle, late teens

However, a drawn-out death is different in some ways, and the loss is different, because the process of death has been different. You've probably received more warning about the impending death. This aspect of the loss changes its impact, it's less of a shock, even if the ultimate result is still a personal tragedy. Weeks, months, or years of warning can give you a chance to accept the forthcoming death, make sense of it, and anticipate the sadness and frustration you'll feel afterward.

Yet a loved one's long illness can cause its own special hardships. A long illness lacks the sheer shock effect of a sudden death, but it can still create tremendous strain.

Family and Personal Stress

If you have a friend or relative who's severely ill, you'll experience anxiety and stress. This will be true even if the situation doesn't add to your personal responsibilities, such as when a friend is the person who's sick. But if you have a sick parent, grandparent, sibling, or other close relative, you may experience even more stress because you may have specific practical duties, such as providing home care for a sick parent. In the meantime, though, your own personal responsibilities haven't disappeared. You still have your own commitments to school, relationships, activities, and interests.

How is it possible to juggle so many demands on your time, energy, patience, and sense of humor? Often it isn't. The other duties that make up your life don't disappear just because of a medical crisis. As a result, a family member's illness probably exerts tremendous stress on your family life. The fatigue alone can be intense. The emotional fatigue is often even worse.

Why the Slow Decline Is So Emotionally Difficult

What about the emotional aspects of a loved one's slow decline? Those can be difficult, too. Here are some of the issues that can affect you.

Role Reversals

One aspect of a protracted illness that can be especially difficult is the reversal of roles. This situation is most common for teens when it's a parent who's sick. Let's say that your mother has a severe illness. This situation is difficult in its own right, but it's also stressful because you may find yourself helping to care for your parent rather than being cared for by her. In short, your roles (in this case, your parent–child roles) have reversed. The changes involved may be minor and easily accommodated. On the other hand, the changes may be substantial and may cause some strain.

Why are role reversals stressful? One obvious reason is simply the added responsibility you'll have to shoulder. Another has to do with the nature of the roles themselves. You're a young adult now; you have more independence than in the past. You're disengaging emotionally from your parents. That's what happens during adolescence—fair enough. But the truth is, you're still your parents' son or daughter. You retain some sort of bond with your parents even though you're gradually disengaging from your family and moving out into the world. There's a sense of connection even if it's negative, such as in families where teens

> Throughout Mother's illness I was so aware of the reversal of our roles—that while she was sick, she had become increasingly dependent on me, and I couldn't be dependent on her. And I resented this all the time. I'm not supposed to be taking care of her—she's supposed to be taking care of me! Even though I was glad to be doing that for her, and felt total duty to her and desire to do for her, it was the reversal of the natural situation. A child is supposed to be taken care of by her mother, not the other way around. There was nobody to function in the role of loved ones. I mean, nobody was my mother.
>
> —Cynthia

don't get along with their parents. As a result, a role reversal between you and your loved ones can be confusing and stressful.

This situation often forces changes in your attitudes as well as in your actions. (For teens, the changes often concern a parent's serious illness.) "It's very difficult for people to switch roles with their loved ones," according to Carolyn Jaffe, formerly a staff nurse at the Hospice of Metro Denver. "To watch your parents decline and become more childlike, more babyish—that's an awful thing to watch. It's very degrading to watch your parents lose their faculties."[12] These emotional issues are potentially as complex as the practical problems that give rise to them.

To complicate matters, you aren't necessarily the only person involved who feels uncomfortable with this situation. The person you're close to may also find these role changes confusing, awkward, even humiliating. They may express frustration, anxiety, and anger about their misfortunes by complaining to the person closest at hand—you. As Colin Murray Parkes told me in an interview, "Parents may feel resentful that you'd let them down, even though you didn't think you did. This is an accusation which old people sometimes make to the young out of their own sense of helplessness or fear, or out of their grief over the loss of their bodily functions, and so on. They take it out on the family."[13] It's worth keeping in mind that some sick people—especially those suffering from strokes, brain tumors, or other organic (physiological) brain problems—may perceive you and other family members with suspicion or paranoia. Try not to take these attitudes personally. They can't help themselves in this regard any more than they can control other aspects of their illness.

Double-Binds

If you're close to someone who's seriously ill—especially if he or she is dying—you may find that no matter what you do or say, you always feel as if you haven't done or said enough. You visit your loved one at the hospital. You do special chores to help out. You try to be supportive and sympathetic. Yet nothing really seems to make enough of a difference. In fact, you may feel that the harder you try, the more this sick person complains about what you're doing or not doing.

This kind of situation is called a "double-bind." You're darned if you do and darned if you don't. When you try to help but can't fix the situation, it's hard not to feel frustrated by the criticisms of your heartfelt efforts.

Here's what's happening. During a serious illness, people feel miserable and helpless. Pain intensifies these reactions. The movies often portray sick people (even those suffering from terminal illnesses) as calm, noble, even blissful. In fact, most people with serious illnesses feel awful, and they may lash out at those around them—even their "nearest and dearest"— out of frustration, anger, and fear. These outbursts don't mean that you've done anything wrong. On the contrary, you're probably doing as much as you can under the circumstances. But in the middle of a family crises (especially one that has continued for a long time and that may never have a favorable resolution) it's easy to imagine that you're falling short. My advice: do as much as you can but don't beat yourself up for failing to solve all the problems your family faces. Sometimes no one can solve the problems!

In short, double-binds are just part of what happens during a loved one's long illness. This isn't a happy situation, but it's part of reality. Do the best you can, then give yourself a break.

Anxiety and Dread

Depending on the particular situation, your loved one may die right away or after a long time, and the uncertainty of the situation creates an added burden. If you knew that he or she would live only six months, you could plan for that duration. If you knew that six years was the likely time span, you could pace yourself accordingly. But when you lack a sense of what lies before you—a sprint or a marathon—it's difficult, even impossible, to guess the most appropriate response to the situation.

Another complication may be a special kind of anxiety in these situations. You may experience a sense of alarm at the thought of your loved one's approaching death. This feeling is often one you can't consciously identify. At times, however, you may be fully aware of it, even overwhelmed by it. The severity depends on the nature of your relationship with the other person, the circumstances of the illness, and other issues. For a parent, sibling, or other relative, for instance, you may feel powerful anxiety and fear about what's happening.

Living Life "on Hold"

One of the most common feelings that teens and others experience during a loved one's protracted illness is that life is "on hold." The circumstances differ from one family to another. Even under the most favorable circumstances, however, a long medical crisis will disrupt most families. The errands, the expenses, and the physical efforts of caring for a sick person are only part of the disruption. There's also the waiting, the uncertainty. Combined, these factors often produce the sensation that life is in limbo.

Mark experienced this situation when his brother Matt developed a blood cancer called multiple myeloma. (Mark was thirteen when Matt was diagnosed at age fifteen.) Matt required complex medical treatments and long hospitalizations, some of which occurred in cities far from the family's home. The brothers' mom, Cindy, spent most of her time attending to the sick teenager; the dad, Alan, continued his work as a lawyer to support the family and pay Matt's growing medical bills. As it turned out, Matt survived for almost twenty-four months after his initial diagnosis. Mark feels that the efforts on his behalf were all worthwhile, but those two years seemed endless.

> We did what we could. We knew from the start that this situation wouldn't have a happy ending because multiple myeloma is incurable. But we all wanted Matt to live as long as possible. So we were sort of in suspended animation. Our family life hinged on the next set of tests and the next round of chemotherapy and the next hospitalization.
>
> —Mark, fifteen

What made the situation rough for Mark wasn't just the knowledge that he'd lose his brother but also the grinding, exhausting journey toward that loss. This is the sort of situation in which anyone would feel a jumble of emotions. A slow decline leaves you riding a roller coaster. You feel hope, despair, sadness, elation, fear, bewilderment, and many other emotions, one after another, sometimes several at once, as your loved one's illness progresses. Sometimes it's hard to know what to feel. Particularly when a disease has an erratic course—bad days and good days, crises and resolutions—the emotional effects can be dizzying. The ups and downs are exhausting. For many people, the early months of intense feelings give way to a kind of numbness. It's too late for blind optimism but too early for grief.

Most people feel frustrated when dealing with the situations we've discussed—responsibilities, medical issues, role reversals, and so forth—and when dealing with their limbo-like consequences. Unfortunately, many of these situations don't lend themselves to easy solutions. There are, however, a variety of resources that can make your situation less exhausting and troublesome than if you try to deal with it alone. (See chapter 5 for ways to find help in dealing with these crises. Also check chapter 9, the resource guide.)

The Aftermath of a Slow Decline

If your loved one dies following a slow decline, you'll probably feel less severely shocked or bewildered than you would have felt following a more sudden loss. You've probably anticipated what will happen, and you may even be ready for it. This is especially likely if your loved one is elderly or if your loved one (whether young or old) has been ill for many years. The emotions involved aren't necessarily mild or short-lived. However, bereavement following a loved one's slow decline is often more straightforward than what follows a sudden death.

You're less likely to double back, psychologically speaking, on the event itself; you're less likely to question whether it has occurred.

One possible explanation for this phenomenon is what bereavement experts call "anticipatory grieving." Many researchers believe that grief can start and progress long before a death occurs. The diagnosis, medical tests and procedures, changes in appearance and behavior, and other events during the loved one's illness all trigger thoughts and emotions about impending loss.

> When there is knowledge . . . that death is probable, or inevitable in the near future, those who are to be affected may grieve to some degree beforehand.
> —Beverley Raphael,
> *The Anatomy of Bereavement*[14]

Another aspect of this issue goes a step farther. The relative lack of shock following a loved one's slow decline isn't simply a matter of your accepting the inevitable death in advance of its occurrence. It also involves what you may have done during that time. Perhaps you've been either directly or indirectly involved in your loved one's care. Perhaps you've spent time together during the illness. Such involvement is often difficult and upsetting, yet it can also provide unexpected satisfactions. The chance to help that person, to offer encouragement, to ease his or her suffering, often becomes a source of reassurance and consolation for everyone.

Perhaps most important, the slow decline can allow you and your loved ones a final chance for closeness or reconciliation. Herbert Hendin, a psychiatrist at New York's Metropolitan Hospital, describes how this can come about. "That period [during a loved one's illness] can be an opportunity—strange as

> One of the few things that was good about that time was realizing that I helped my mom suffer a little less than what might have happened. I still feel bad about what she went through. I'm not saying I did something better than what other people did. But I did what I could. And she would have been worse off if I hadn't.
> —Meera, eighteen

it may sound—to try to deal with certain issues with the loved one."[15] Strong bonds can grow still stronger. Weak relationships can heal. You may be able to overcome long-lasting estrangements. Your loved one's illness, no matter how tragic, can become a final chance to develop together within your relationship.

What happens is rarely simple or straightforward. For most people, a loved one's slow decline is a time of anguish, confusion, and fatigue. Yet even under difficult circumstances, many sons and daughters value the final months or years of helping their loved ones despite the difficulties. Sometimes a loved one's slow decline is simply an event to endure. For others, the passage of time lets a sense of meaning emerge.

The remaining chapters of this book will address these and other issues.

NOTES

1. Beverley Raphael, *The Anatomy of Bereavement* (New York: Basic Books, 1983), 54.

2. Colin Murray Parkes and Robert S. Weiss, *Recovery from Bereavement* (New York: Basic Books, 1983), 71.

3. Raphael, *The Anatomy of Bereavement,* 56.

4. Parkes and Weiss, *Recovery from Bereavement,* 73.

5. Raphael, *The Anatomy of Bereavement,* 57.

6. Raphael, *The Anatomy of Bereavement,* 59.

7. Raphael, *The Anatomy of Bereavement,* 63.

8. Evelyn Gladu, private interview.

9. John Nagel, private interview.

10. Aleta Koman, private interview.

11. Edwin Bokert, private interview.

12. Carolyn Jaffe, private interview.

13. Colin Murray Parkes, private interview.

14. Raphael, *The Anatomy of Bereavement,* 67.

15. Herbert Hendin, private interview.

4 Other Ways Loss and Grief Can Affect You

Grief is normal, but that doesn't mean it isn't confusing, frustrating, or painful. If you can anticipate and understand some of the consequences of grief, however, you'll be better able to deal with them. We discussed some effects of grief in chapters 2 and 3. Here are some other ways in which loss and bereavement can change your life.

FAMILY CHANGES

The previous chapter suggested at one point that certain events following a loved one's death can strain relationships with family members. For teenagers, this situation probably happens most often following a parent's death. The reason isn't hard to identify: a parent's death changes your family's structure and the ways in which you and the other family members interact. The death of a brother or sister

The particular human chain we're part of is central to our individual identity.
—Elizabeth Stone, American writer[1]

can also have profound consequences for the whole family. A grandparent's or other relative's death may have similar, powerful effects. In any of these instances, the death can change your family in ways that go far beyond the loss of a single member.

New Closeness

A death in the family can be a major turning point for the survivors. Sometimes tremendous growth occurs—family members may set aside long-standing differences or express

their love more openly. Shared loss can inspire you to work toward deepening or strengthening your relationships. These insights and the changes they can produce are among the great consolations following a parent's death.

As Mindy, age sixteen, stated following her grandmother's death, "I wasn't particularly close to Gram, but her death last year really shook me up because I saw how much it upset my mom. That did something: it showed me how hard it could be to lose a parent. I started thinking a little more about what it could be like to lose my own parents. So I'd say overall that I feel closer now to Mom and Dad, especially Mom."

What's most important is to stay open to changes within your relationships. New closeness is valuable in its own right. Just keep in mind that old attitudes and roles are durable; change may take years to occur.

Estrangements

A parent's or other relative's death can also strain your relationships with other family members. Sometimes these changes in relationships are temporary—perhaps a side effect of tensions during or right after a family crisis. At other times, they are the start of permanent estrangement.

What accounts for these disruptions? Why would family members who have already suffered one loss make matters worse by squabbling, holding grudges, or expressing resentments? There are many possible explanations, some of which are specific to individual families. But there are some general reasons as well.

> I thought my dad's death would bring my family closer together, but it didn't. Far from it. My brothers and I fought over everything—the funeral arrangements, decisions about financial stuff, chores, meals, everything. We didn't get along too great before Dad died and afterwards was even worse.
>
> —Michael, nineteen

One reason is that loss and bereavement are private experiences in many ways, and their emotional effects on individuals are unpredictable. You and your family members share a sense of loss, but the person who died has a different meaning for each person within your family. Since each family member has an individual way of feeling and expressing his or her own sense of loss, these differences may cause conflicts instead of harmony, isolation instead of closeness.

Suppose that your father has died. You are mourning the loss of a parent. Meanwhile, your mother is mourning the

"Often your remaining parent or relative isn't emotionally available because of his or her own grief," according to John Nagel, MD, a psychiatrist in Fort Collins, Colorado. "Another possibility is that your parent may be more focused on a younger child in the family." What's the result of these situations? You may end up grieving on your own. Dr. Nagel suggests that if you feel emotionally isolated by this kind of situation, you may tend to become excessively self-reliant as a response. "This may make it harder for you to ask for help later. So, go ahead and remember to rely on others. Find someone reliable who can listen to you."[2]

loss of her spouse. Both losses are emotionally difficult, but they are different losses in many ways. You have lost the man who helped to create you and nurture you; your mother has lost the man she chose to be her mate. Although you've shared certain experiences that your father and her husband brought to each of you, your sense of him will be drastically different. Even the experiences you shared will have different meanings for each of you.

In addition, the *practical* effects of the loss will differ. As a teenager, you may experience some practical consequences, such as changes in your financial situation, following the death of a parent. The death of your parent will have even more severe consequences for your other parent—not just the loss of income but also the loss of his or her marriage partner. In the aftermath of a loss, when stress is high and energy is low, it's often difficult to remember how differently people grieve the

What can you do to help yourself? Here are several responses that can make a difference:

- Look after your own bereavement. You have your own loss to grieve. If you ignore your health, your feelings, your school tasks, your friendships, and other aspects of your life, you'll limit how much you can help others.
- At the same time, try to be there, if possible, for your other family members. "Being there" doesn't mean that you should respond to every request or demand that people make of you. But try to remember that grief creates difficult transitions for everyone. Your family members' grief will take time to resolve.
- Recognize the limits of what you can do to help. You can be sympathetic and supportive, but you can't take away someone else's pain. Ultimately, your family members must mourn their own losses.
- If necessary, get support for yourself—and suggest separate support for your parent. Counseling or a bereavement group can help you and your surviving parent.

death of the same person. The fact that both you and your surviving parent are both bereaved doesn't necessarily mean that you're having the same experience. Likewise, sharing a loss won't necessarily mean that each of you is the best person to help one another. My recommendation: consider seeking support from people outside your immediate family. An uncle or aunt, a trusted teacher or counselor, or a therapist may be helpful. See chapter 6 for further suggestions.

In addition, keep an eye open to the possibility that your family members may not deal successfully with bereavement. The death of a husband or wife can cause serious difficulties for the surviving spouse. The death of a sibling will be difficult for you but perhaps even harder on your parents. If your mother, father, or siblings develop severe problems following a death in the family, you may need to alert some other relatives to what's happening. The specific points of concern are:

- Prolonged inability to believe that the death has occurred
- Prolonged social isolation following the death
- Inability to care for herself or himself
- Reliance on alcohol or drugs to relieve a sense of anguish, loneliness, guilt, or other emotions
- Extensive changing of plans or making of decisions according to what her or his spouse would have preferred, rather than according to personal preferences
- Great effort to *avoid* thinking of the spouse
- Substantial weight gain, weight loss, or marked deterioration of health
- Suicidal thoughts or gestures, or attempted suicide
- Inability to "get on" with life, to invest energy in living.[3]

How well your family members are dealing with bereavement is often hard to determine. If you have any major doubts, raise the issue with relatives you trust. They may be able to locate resources that can help the members of your immediate family.

Sibling Conflicts

Conflicts among brothers and sisters are common and generally normal. Although it's not unusual for brothers and sisters to get along during a parent's illness and after the death, it's also a common occurrence for siblings to end up arguing or resenting each other. Excessively high expectations of brotherly/sisterly love may complicate the situation. The truth of the matter: although it sounds strange, you and your siblings may be the last people capable of helping each other. This isn't *despite* the shared loss but *because* of it. Why? Because you and your siblings are suffering the same loss. You're probably experiencing similar anxieties and stresses.

You're physically or emotionally depleted in the same ways. Why should you be the perfect allies during your recovery from grief? What each of you wants and needs—patience, clear perspective, abundant energy, and an optimistic outlook—is precisely what each of you lacks.

In addition, your parent's illness and death may evoke long-forgotten (or perhaps well-remembered!) sibling competition and resentment. Dr. Raphael believes that "the conflicts may be reawakened from sibling conflicts of rivalry and envy in early childhood. The death seems to highlight what has had to be shared in caring for the parent and what burdens must be

What should you do about these conflicts? Here are a few suggestions:

- Remember that grief heightens emotions. You and your siblings are under stress, and your reactions even to everyday events may be more intense than usual. What seem like hopeless problems may look easier to solve in a few months. Don't burn your bridges.
- Consider the possibility of an outsider's viewpoint. You and your siblings may have such strong feelings about the aftermath of a death in the family that you may not be able to see events clearly. A trusted aunt, uncle, other relative, or family friend may be able to provide insights that all of you lack.
- Be careful of speaking your mind too impulsively. Bereavement can provide an opportunity for speaking with rare candor—an opportunity often well worth taking. However, ultimatums, dares, and threats made during a time of confusion may drastically compound the damage your family has already suffered.

borne, and also who feels responsible."[4] Powerful old feelings combine with the more immediate tensions. The result is a strain on sibling relationships. It's not surprising that brothers and sisters have difficulties getting along when parents die.

CHANGES IN OTHER RELATIONSHIPS

The death in your family may affect your relationships with other people as well. Interactions with other relatives may improve or worsen, and your friendships may improve or deteriorate during your bereavement.

Between You and Your Friends

Friendship ties are different from family bonds, but grief can affect them intensely. The difficulties you face in dealing with a family tragedy can strongly influence these relationships. Some friends may rally and be supportive. Others may feel confused about how to respond and withdraw from you. As Sue put it, "You do find out who your *real* friends are! The desire of most of my 'friends' not to talk with me about Mom's death was very hard to deal with. I even had one such 'friend' sever our relationship totally!"

What about improvements in your friendships? This can happen, too. During her mother's illness and after the death, Lisa found that many friends, especially girls, tried to be supportive and nurturing. "Sometimes they almost gave me too much support," says Lisa, "but it meant a lot to me that they tried. I didn't feel so alone."

The suggestions I made earlier about changes in family relationships sometimes apply to these friendships as well—at least to some extent. Loss and grief can change friendships, but the effects diminish over time. Over the next few months and years, your relationships with friends will probably return to a more balanced state. It's a real loss when friendships fall by the wayside, but some friendships may grow stronger even if others weaken. Either way, the changes aren't entirely your choice. Your friends must make some sort of effort, too, in understanding and accepting the changes in your life.

All Quiet?

One other possibility: perhaps, following a loved one's death, no relationships will change at all, or will change just a little. Maybe you won't grow much closer to your family members *or* grow apart. Maybe your friendships will stay fairly

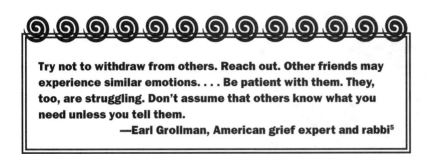

> Try not to withdraw from others. Reach out. Other friends may experience similar emotions. . . . Be patient with them. They, too, are struggling. Don't assume that others know what you need unless you tell them.
> —Earl Grollman, American grief expert and rabbi[5]

stable. There's certainly no reason for you to feel that changes in relationships are inevitable following a loved one's death. If this sense of calm is what you experience, count yourself lucky and move on.

PERSONAL CHANGES

Just as grief can change your relationships, it can create personal changes, too. Loss shakes you up and changes how you see yourself and your place in the world. This "shake-up" isn't fun or easy, but you're better off acknowledging that it's possible than pretending that it doesn't exist.

Cultural Discomfort with Grief

Americans are often uncomfortable with bereavement. In many other cultures, people have more leeway to express their grief—to cry, to dress in special ways that signify mourning, to withdraw from daily life for a while. In our society, however, we do our best to ignore bereavement. Death and loss are still fairly uncomfortable subjects for many Americans.

These cultural attitudes may complicate your feelings during the grief process. You may feel pressure from other people to grieve in one way rather than another. You may start to wonder if your own emotions are inappropriate or excessive. ("If people think grief is no big deal, why am I so upset?")

The dilemma is slightly different depending on your gender. Our culture generally lets girls and women express their emotions more openly than it allows boys and men. In this

sense, girls and women have more "room" to grieve. Boys and men are more likely to keep their feelings under the surface. But too many people, both male and female, have experienced other people's impatience about their grief.

One of the best ways for dealing with this situation is to find at least one real confidant or close buddy who can accept the complexities of your bereavement. Although a good friend or a relative is ideal, sometimes your close friends may be almost *too* close. This may also be true with a brother or sister, who may be too emotionally involved in his or her grief to understand your own. A friend who has also experienced loss, perhaps even the loss of a parent, seems more promising.

> People were pretty open about what I felt right after Mom died. Nobody got annoyed at me if I cried. But after a few weeks I got the feeling I'd "worn out my welcome." I didn't even have to cry—I'd just feel kind of lonely from missing her, and people could tell, and some weren't very patient. As if I should get over my mother's death in five or six weeks!
> —Jenn, seventeen

Girls probably have the advantage here. Generally speaking, boys have fewer friends with whom they can discuss emotional issues than girls do. Most of the boys who have told me about experiencing intense grief reactions mentioned their mother as the person who was most supportive. Other boys found their sisters to be helpful. Unfortunately, few boys described their brothers or male friends as sensitive toward their situations or even open about the situation. Quite the contrary, friends often seemed at a loss over how to deal with a boy's bereavement. But there are alternatives. See chapter 5 for suggestions.

What matters most is this: remember that you have a right to feel what you feel. You have the right to take your time grieving the death of your loved one.

Memories

The death of someone you love often releases a flood of memories. Images, incidents, bits of conversation, shapeless feelings, and sometimes even hallucinations rush forth. If your relationship with the other person was negative, then the memories may be negative too. But even if the relationship was happy, the sheer abundance and intensity of memories may seem overwhelming.

In the aftermath of a frightening crisis, you may also find that the events you witnessed—your loved one's helplessness, frustration, and pain—now haunts you. You may worry that the experience of watching that person suffer and die will displace your memories of the good times shared in the past.

These worries are common, normal, and understandable. It's frightening to think that recent events might end up more vivid than the long happy years preceding.

If you've experienced a situation that causes bad memories, you can rest assured that the painful recollections will ease. The vividness of your loved one's suffering will dim; the images of dying and death will fade. This isn't to say that you'll entirely forget what he or she went through. But the intense, ugly memories that often linger following a death will diminish both in intensity and in frequency. More important, your earlier sense of the person you loved—your sense of him or her as vibrant and capable and happy—will return. Your recollections of good times and loving relationships are ultimately more powerful than the hardships that ended them.

> My mom went into a coma after three brain surgeries and never revived. It was worse than the worst situation I'd ever imagined—she couldn't get well but she couldn't seem to die, either. We had to put her in a nursing home. She stayed there fourteen months and that seemed to go on forever.
> —Francisco, eighteen

Holidays and Anniversaries

Following a loved one's death, you may also experience some difficulty during holidays and anniversaries. This isn't surprising: after all, these occasions are times of intense emotion even under the best of circumstances; grief will intensify your reactions.

> The anniversary of a death or other anniversaries associated with it may result in reawakened bereavement.
> —Beverley Raphael, Australian psychiatrist[6]

Strong feelings at a particular time of year seem all the more likely if you consider how much you associate certain holidays with your family and close friends. For most Christian families, Christmas and Easter provide the strongest images of family celebration and sharing. Passover, Chanukah, and the high holy days evoke similar feelings for Jews. Thanksgiving, Mother's Day, Father's Day, your loved one's birthday, and the anniversaries of his or her death can also inspire special feelings. Which particular days affect you depends on family tradition, on your willingness to acknowledge your own feelings, and on other individual factors.

How to deal with your emotions at such times is a matter of individual preference. Some people prefer to acknowledge their recollections, others to ignore them. Either response is understandable. It's good to remember, however, that the intensity of recollection is often greatest during the first few years following the death. Don't worry that you'll be awash in emotion during each holiday for the rest of your life. You can indulge your memories without concern for becoming preoccupied. Some families even make a remembrance of the parent part of their celebration.

> Rituals are an important way of saying goodbye. I suggest to families that they create a ritual that can be a way of memorializing the person who died. One way is to take items of symbolic significance—things that mean something to you regarding the person who died—and put them into a box or a bottle. Then throw them into a river or the ocean.
> —John Nagel, MD, American psychiatrist[7]

Emotional Leeway

Looking after yourself during bereavement is more than just a matter of staying rested, fed, and healthy, but treating yourself

> People often think that they should get better quickly, and if they're still feeling bad two months later, there's something wrong with them. Well, that's not true. People need to go at their own pace and in their own way.
> —Wendy Foster-Evans, former director of bereavement, Hospice of Marin, San Rafael, California[8]

well in these ways is a necessary start. In addition, you should give yourself some emotional leeway. Don't expect too much too soon. Bereavement is hard work—and often long work as well. As Marcia Lattanzi, a former grief counselor at the Hospice of Boulder County, Colorado, puts it, "Be gentle with yourself."[8]

The most important thing for you to keep in mind is that you will almost certainly go through the grief process without harm. "Most people deal pretty well with loss," according to American sociologist Robert Weiss, "and most recover uneventfully."[9] You'll not only withstand the stresses of loss—you'll prevail over them as well.

POTENTIAL FOR POSITIVE CHANGE

One of the most remarkable aspects of loss and grief is the potential for positive change in its aftermath. As Colin Murray Parkes stated during our interview, "I happen to believe that most major changes that people face in their lives are both threats to health and also opportunities for growth. The more I study bereavement, the more convinced I become that transcending grief—coming through the process in a healthy way—is a growth-promoting experience, however painful it may be, in the vast majority of people who go through it."[10]

> Healing involves being willing to hurt more now in order to someday hurt less. It is the process of going through—not over, around, or under—your pain.
> —Earl Grollman[11]

These changes don't mean that the process isn't painful. As I've said throughout this book, grief almost always involves pain. Grief also goes hand in hand with tasks that can be difficult to accomplish. Just because bereavement can bring positive changes doesn't mean that you won't deeply regret your loved one's death and grieve that person's absence from your life. But the potential for change is there. Many people experience it, and the benefits are often long lasting.

Does this mean that you should necessarily find grief a positive, transformative experience? Not at all. Some people do;

some don't. Sometimes it's just a hard time to get through. Feeling negative about bereavement doesn't mean that something's wrong with you. It means simply that the circumstances of your relationships, or the particular task you've faced, have been too demanding or exhausting to allow for more positive side effects.

However, if you feel creative change taking place following the loss you've experienced, there's nothing wrong with your attitude. It's a relief to have the crisis over. It's great to get on with your own life again. It's a source of pride to learn from a difficult experience and move on.

NOTES

1. See www.quotationspage.com.
2. John Nagel, private interview.
3. Grollman, *Straight Talk about Death for Teenagers: How to Cope with Losing Someone You Love* (Boston: Beacon, 1993), 58.
4. Beverley Raphael, *The Anatomy of Bereavement* (New York: Basic Books, 1983), 84.
5. Grollman, *Strait Talk about Death for Teenagers*, 58.

6. Raphael, *The Anatomy of Bereavement*, 62.
7. John Nagel, private interview.
8. Wendy Foster-Evans, private interview.
9. Marcia Lattanzi, private interview.
10. Robert S. Weiss, private interview.
11. Colin Murray Parkes, private interview.
12. Grollman, *Straight Talk about Death for Teenagers*, 58.

5

What Helps during Bereavement

Grief is inevitable—it's just part of being human. Grief is difficult—there's no way of just wishing it away. There's no way out of it but *through* it. If there's no easy solution to the problem, what can you do about it? Should you just put up with the grief process and wait for it to ease? Or are there steps you can take to help yourself?

In fact, you can be active in coping with loss and grief, and doing so can make bereavement relatively easier and often a less unhappy experience. This chapter and the next offer a variety of suggestions for how you can ease the pain of grief.

ALLOW YOURSELF TO FEEL WHAT YOU'RE FEELING

You have a right to feel the loss you've suffered. You have a right to experience grief in your own individual way. Other people in your family may not be affected as much, or they may be affected more intensely, or they may be affected in different ways. In any case, you shouldn't expect your grief to be exactly like anyone else's, and you should allow yourself to feel what you're feeling.

Let Your Emotions Out

People feel many different emotions during bereavement, and it's okay to express these feelings. Deeply felt emotions are normal in this situation. You may find the intensity of grief alarming, but rest assured that what you're going through is all part of the process. Crying, screaming, laughing, and other intense expressions of grief are not only acceptable but good, as letting your emotions out in these ways are healthy expressions of what you're feeling.

Here's the catch, though: our society is often uncomfortable with grief and its emotional manifestations. Unlike cultures in Latin America, Asia, Africa, and many parts of Europe, where people accept and even encourage intense expressions of bereavement, American culture tends to be more reserved about these emotions. Sometimes you'll even hear folks praise the bereaved for their *lack* of emotion— "She's so dignified despite her pain," or "He's being so strong." Do these comments mean that *not* expressing grief is better than expressing it? No. Do they mean that you should "hold yourself together" and stifle your grief-stricken tears, screams, or laughter? Not at all.

What I suggest is that you pick the right time and place. Our culture accepts

I'm not very religious. I haven't felt very connected to my religion for a long time. But the services at my church after my little sister died were a good thing because I could cry and be upset and not feel there was something wrong with me. Everyone there was very supportive.

—Antoine, eighteen

the expression of intense feelings at a funeral or memorial service, but those events take up only a small period of time during the overall grief process. What about the other weeks or months (or longer) when you feel intensely bereaved? I suggest that you find a time

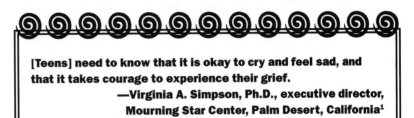

[Teens] need to know that it is okay to cry and feel sad, and that it takes courage to experience their grief.
—Virginia A. Simpson, Ph.D., executive director, Mourning Star Center, Palm Desert, California[1]

and place when you can either be alone or with people you trust—people who will accept you, embrace you, and let you express whatever is in your heart during such a difficult time.

Listen to Music, Sing, or Play Your Favorite Instrument

For thousands of years, human beings have vented their emotions—delight, fear, longing, and grief—through music. I encourage you to do the same. No matter what sort of music you enjoy, it can be a source of great comfort and release. Perhaps what helps you is listening to CDs of your favorite performers.

Whenever you think about the person you lost, go and listen to some music that you like.
—Aundrea, thirteen

Perhaps you play an instrument. Perhaps you like to sing. The way you use music makes no difference; it's a great "escape hatch" no matter what your preferences. Perhaps it allows you to go deeper into your grief or to escape your sadness and sense of loss—either way is fine.

Write Poetry

Similarly, you can use poetry as a wonderful release. You don't have to write a literary masterpiece; just put your feelings onto paper. Write down what you appreciated about your loved one. Write about what you miss. Write what you're feeling now

> **All sorrows can be borne if you put them into a story or tell a story about them.**
>
> **—Isak Dinesen, Danish writer[2]**

that he or she is gone. Expect this process to be intense—after all, you're digging deep into your emotions. Even if the process is painful at the time, however, you'll almost certainly feel better if you allow yourself this release.

Write in a Journal

Another way to explore and express your feelings is to keep a journal of thoughts, memories, and experiences. Write by free association, noting whatever thoughts or feelings you experience. Try not to inhibit what you think or feel. Write as honestly and as clearly as possible, without feeling that you have to hide anything or that your emotions are embarrassing or shameful. Note any thoughts or feelings of rage, anger, frustration. Don't censor anything, especially events and feelings that make you feel uncomfortable.

Writing in a journal is one of the best ways to vent your emotions, but it serves another purpose as well: capturing your recollections of your loved one. As Virginia A. Simpson of the Mourning Star Center puts it, "I also recommend writing down their memories of the person who died because even though they think they will remember, as time goes on, memories fade."

Keeping an uncensored, uninhibited journal is a good way to release your most intimate emotions. It's cheap, safe, and harmless to yourself and other people. Precisely because the

> **A mourner is . . . a person with a story. The pity is how very rarely it gets told.**
>
> **—Christian McEwen, English poet and writer[3]**

topics you describe are so intimate, however, *make sure that you can maintain your privacy.* Put the journal in a place where no one else can find it. Find somewhere that's safe enough that you don't have to worry about discovery. Once you've written your entries, you may end up having an experience that crystallizes your insights; later, you may decide to destroy or discard the journal. That's fine, too. Think of the journal as a *process,* not a *product.*

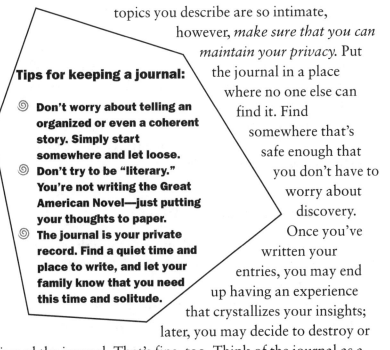

Tips for keeping a journal:

- Don't worry about telling an organized or even a coherent story. Simply start somewhere and let loose.
- Don't try to be "literary." You're not writing the Great American Novel—just putting your thoughts to paper.
- The journal is your private record. Find a quiet time and place to write, and let your family know that you need this time and solitude.

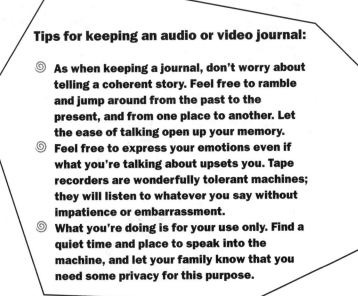

Tips for keeping an audio or video journal:

- As when keeping a journal, don't worry about telling a coherent story. Feel free to ramble and jump around from the past to the present, and from one place to another. Let the ease of talking open up your memory.
- Feel free to express your emotions even if what you're talking about upsets you. Tape recorders are wonderfully tolerant machines; they will listen to whatever you say without impatience or embarrassment.
- What you're doing is for your use only. Find a quiet time and place to speak into the machine, and let your family know that you need some privacy for this purpose.

Record an Audio or Video "Journal"

An alternative to use of a journal is recording your thoughts with a tape recorder or camcorder. This method can accomplish many of the same goals as using a journal: creating a window into your experiences, helping you remember events, and assisting you in understanding yourself. As with a written journal, however, it's crucial that you protect your privacy. The journal you create is for you alone.

Paint, Draw, Scribble, or Doodle

Some people prefer the visual image to the written word. If that sounds like you, art can be a wonderful way of expressing your emotions. Here again, you don't have to emulate Rembrandt or Picasso to experience something worthwhile. Just let out what you're feeling. Even the wildest, most unformed scribbles can serve you well as you wrestle with the chaotic emotions you have inside. The goal isn't to create a work of art, only to express your grief.

Find Solace in Spirituality

If you are religious or spiritually inclined, you can find great solace in your traditions or personal practices. Expressing your emotions in this way may mean prayer, or it may involve taking part in the liturgies of your religion. People who aren't members of a formal tradition can find reassurance in spiritual practices too. Meditation is one option. Physical disciplines such as hatha yoga, t'ai chi, and qi gong can offer solace during a time of sadness and upheaval. Even taking a walk in the woods or along the beach can offer a sense of spiritual connection and reassurance. (I'll have more to say about these physical expressions of grief later in this chapter.)

PAMPER YOURSELF

It's easy to forget that grief is hard work. When you lose someone you love, it's a huge blow to your physical and emotional well-being. You may feel unusually tired or moody. You may feel hungrier than usual, or less hungry. You may need more sleep. For these reasons, I strongly recommend that you pamper yourself during bereavement. Self-indulgent? Not at all. If you give yourself some extra leeway to deal with the stresses you face, you'll cope with the situation better, adjust more quickly, and be less likely to experience problematic grief.

Some good ways to pamper yourself:

Slow Down

Modern life puts us all under tremendous pressure. We race around too much, doing too many things at once. Unfortunately, grief increases the pressure we feel. One response: try to slow down. Avoid making too many

I don't think I ever felt so tired in my life [following his father's death]. I felt like I ran a marathon every single day.
—Jackson, seventeen

commitments when you're emotionally depleted and perhaps physically exhausted as well. Live your life at a slower pace until you regain your emotional balance. Does this mean you skip school, ignore your family chores, or withdraw from your friends? No—simply that you take care not to run yourself down at a time when you're already stressed. Pace yourself. Don't commit yourself to additional activities that may wear you out. Take it easy.

Give Yourself Some TLC

Another way to pamper yourself is to give yourself an emotional or sensory treat now and then. Buy yourself a new CD. Go see a movie. Take a long bath instead of a quick shower. If you like sports, visit a gym, a skating rink, a water park, a climbing wall, or some other place where you can let loose physically. Find other methods to indulge yourself in other easy, safe, affordable ways.

Indulge Your Senses

Some phases of the grief process can leave you feeling washed out, empty, and depressed. That's part of what happens, and you can't really make it go away just by force of will. At the same time, it's possible to limit the emptiness you feel by replenishing yourself in certain ways. One of these ways is to indulge your senses—to give yourself sensory stimulation that reminds you of the richness and abundance of life. We've already discussed how music can be nourishing. You can indulge your sense of smell, too, by providing yourself with lush fragrances you enjoy: foods, flowers, scented candles, perfumes or aftershave lotions—whatever appeals to you. The sense of taste? That's easy: treat yourself to the meals and occasional snacks that you enjoy. (Don't "drown your cares in food," which is a temptation that can easily backfire. But selecting foods you like is important.) The sense of touch? I've already mentioned long baths, which is one of the cheapest, most relaxing forms of self-indulgence available. If you can afford it,

consider getting a professional massage now and then—a great
way to ease tension. If that option is too expensive, consider
exchanging back rubs with your family members.

Eat Right

Grief can do a real number on your appetite. Like other
severe shocks to your emotional balance, losing someone you
love can leave you in a state in which you either aren't hungry
or else you simply forget to eat. This situation is
understandable, and it's okay to eat less than what you need *for
a brief period of time,* but it's not a good thing for more than a
short while. Especially if it goes on for more than a day or two,
a suppressed appetite can leave you tired, weak, and vulnerable
to colds and other illnesses. Skipping meals can also leave you
feeling depressed.

My recommendation: make sure you eat right. Again, this
doesn't mean overeating; it's not possible to "eat your way out
of bereavement." On the contrary, you should make sure that
you're getting the foods you really need—enough protein, a
sensible amount of carbohydrates, and plenty of fruits and
vegetables. Be sure to drink enough water, too. If you eat a
good diet, you're more likely to maintain your stamina during
the ups and downs of the grief process.

Get Extra Sleep

Similarly, you're going to need some extra sleep. It's not
uncommon for people to experience sleep loss during
bereavement. The shock of losing a loved one is often so

The first few weeks after my sister died, I forgot to eat or else
had no appetite. I just didn't think about food. Once I started
eating again, I realized that part of my low mood and low
energy was "running on empty."

—Geri, fifteen

disturbing that you find it more difficult to fall asleep and, even when you doze off, it may be harder to stay asleep. Don't be worried if you experience disrupted sleep, especially in the early phases of the grief process. Once things settle down, though, it's possible that you'll feel extra tired as you adjust to your loss. You may sleep longer than usual but wake up feeling exhausted. You may also feel drowsy at odd times of day.

How should you respond? There's no easy answer to this question, but bereavement experts routinely suggest making sure that you get lots of sleep during this difficult time. Given the nature of teenagers' school schedules, this may mean going to bed a little earlier than usual, since it may not be feasible to get up any later. You may also want to catch a nap once you get home from school. There's nothing wrong with indulging yourself in some extra sleep, and it can only work to your advantage in the long run.

Take Care of Your Health

If someone you love has died, you may feel that your own health issues are trivial by comparison. But you shouldn't neglect your physical well-being during bereavement. Fatigue alone can cause health problems or aggravate preexisting conditions. Emotional stress can harm your health. Since fatigue and stress are common during the grief process, you may become vulnerable to illness. This doesn't mean that you'll develop a terrible disease; however, you should be attentive to

your physical and mental well-being after a major loss. If you're concerned about yourself, get a checkup. Your family doctor will probably give you a clean bill of health, and the good news will take that much worry off your mind.

Do Something Fun

Another way to pamper yourself: have some fun! You may resist this idea, for you may feel that it's inappropriate, even insulting, to the memory of the person you've lost. That's a common worry among the bereaved. How can you indulge yourself in fun activities when the person you loved is dead?! Well, as the saying goes, life is for the living. Is it likely that your loved one would really want you to put yourself "on hold"? It's far more likely that he or she would prefer that you move on when you're ready, savor the richness of experience, and relish the joys of living. So—enjoy yourself. Go play in the park. Fly a kite. Go swimming. Ride your bike. Hang out with friends. Visit an amusement park. Go see a movie. Delight in the world around you.

EXERT YOURSELF

One of the best ways to lessen the burden of grief is to get out and *move*. Action is beneficial in many ways. First of all, it's good for your body to get regular exercise anyway. Second, physical activity can help you break away from constant preoccupations with the loss you've suffered. Third, aerobic exercise releases the brain's endorphins, natural chemicals that create a sense of well-being. These benefits won't make grief go away, but they can diminish the side effects that make bereavement so difficult.

Sports

What's your favorite sport? Almost any activity you enjoy can have positive effects on you during bereavement. Team sports may be especially helpful, since they have the double advantage of combining physical exertion with group dynamics. But almost any sport that gets you up and moving works to your advantage. (One possible concern: if you're really exhausted because of the grief you're feeling, take it easy at first. Don't do too much too soon. Also, give yourself some leeway as you practice your sport, since you may be less focused than usual and therefore less accomplished at whatever sport you're playing.)

The only cure for grief is action.
—George Henry Lewes, English philosopher, literary critic, and scientist[4]

Walking Just for the Sake of Walking

I urge you to get up and out. Take a hike. Walk in the woods or in your local park. If the conditions are safe, a solitary walk can provide both some exercise and some quality time with your own thoughts. If it's safer or more appealing to have some company, take a walk with a good friend, which offers the double advantages of activity and companionship.

Other Forms of Exercise

Even if you're not avid about sports, or if you just can't muster the energy for organized or competitive activities, you have many alternatives to choose from. Go jogging in the park. Go swimming in the local pool. Take a ride on your bike. Just get moving, stretch out, and shake off the tension.

One of the best things for me [after her mother's death] was walking. Nobody could bother me, I liked being outdoors, and I always felt better afterwards.
—Samantha, eighteen

Other options include various Eastern physical disciplines and forms of creative movement—such as yoga, t'ai chi, and dance. Hatha yoga can help you stay in shape, relax your body, and calm your mind. The same is true for t'ai chi, qi gong, and other Chinese disciplines. I recommend dance as well—any kind of dance that allows you to vent some energy and let loose harmlessly.

FIND SOLACE IN NATURE

Go outside! Many people find consolation in the natural world—in the presence of wildlife, the wind in the trees, the play of light and shadow, the clouds overhead, the shift of the seasons. Seeking comfort in nature won't take away your loss, but it can provide a feeling of connection with the great cycles of life that contain our personal human dramas. In addition, the beauty of the natural world can offer reassurance in its own right.

What kind of experiences seem to help? That depends on what you enjoy and what settings are accessible in your area. Obvious choices include walking along the beach, hiking in the woods, canoeing or sailing on a lake, or bicycling through a local park. Just sitting in your own backyard can provide opportunities to commune with nature. Almost anything will do. Watch a sunrise or sunset. Stare at the stars at night. Observe birds at the bird feeder. Visit a nature preserve or even a zoo.

Another option: seek the company of trusted pets. Dogs and cats often sense when family members are upset and can provide patient, nonjudgmental affection (and a warm critter to hug) during a difficult time.

MEMORIALIZE THE PERSON WHO DIED

It's worthwhile to take steps that help you feel that your experience of the person won't be lost forever. Memorializing your loved one can help you come to terms with loss and preserve a sense of the time you shared. Here are some suggestions:

Do Something to Honor Your Loved One

One of the best ways to do what I'm suggesting is to have some sort of social occasion to remember the person who died. Of course, funerals and memorial services often serve this purpose, as do such rituals as the Catholic wake and the Jewish ritual of *sitting shiva*. But many families don't practice these customs, and sometimes an occasion *in addition to* the formal religious practices can be useful and helpful.

One possibility is to borrow a custom from the Society of Friends—the Quakers. For centuries, the Quakers have memorialized the dead in a way that people from other traditions can adapt to their own purposes, in accordance with their own beliefs, and in their own style. The ceremony involves a gathering of relatives and friends who, following an initial period of silence, take turns recalling that person and what he or she meant to them, to their families, to the community. In addition to acknowledging the person's death, this custom celebrates the life and its effects on the living.

> After Dad died, we held a private memorial service a few days after the public funeral. Only family members and close friends attended. We sat around in the living room, ate the goodies that people brought, and told stories about Dad. Everyone contributed. This was *so* different from the funeral—we could say anything we wanted without "saying the right thing," and we could tell "the whole story" about Dad. I learned a lot of things about him I'd never known before! We laughed, we cried, we sang. Everyone there could remember Dad in their own way, and none of us will ever forget that night.
>
> —Liz, seventeen

Another option is simply to throw a party. You can invite friends and family, offer them food, and provide an opportunity to share memories and remember the good times you had with your loved one. This kind of occasion both memorializes the person who died and gives others a chance to express their own emotions about what has happened. You may find it healing to hear other people describe your loved one—stories about his or her talents, interests, life experiences, and foibles.

Gather a Few Keepsakes

Another idea: gather up some keepsakes and preserve them for the future. Some families I know have sorted photographs, selected especially memorable ones, and created albums for posterity. What's creative about this process isn't just the act of making the album; it's the reminiscing and discussion that are central parts of the project. Other families divide up personal effects—a parent's knickknacks, a sibling's favorite sports equipment, a grandparent's mementos—so that each member of the family has something to remember that person by. The goal isn't to create a "shrine" to the person who died; rather, it's to have a special item or two that can serve as a reminder of someone you've loved.

Write a Letter

Earlier, I mentioned that writing poetry or a journal can be great ways to vent your emotions during bereavement. It's also a way to remember the person you've lost. Another method of delving into the past involves writing letters. Letter writing is both a way of memorializing your loved one and saying good-bye. The goal is to release thoughts and feelings about your own past.

To use this method, you write a letter to a specific person (your mother, father, siblings, or whomever) and say whatever you may have left unsaid. The words you write can express disappointment, anger, frustration, grief—whatever you're feeling. It doesn't matter how hostile or hurtful your words, since the "recipient" of your letter will never receive it anyway. The point is simply to vent what you're feeling—to get it off your chest. In doing so, the anxiety, fear, and anger you've experienced can surge outward rather than remain submerged, which can help you move on and find more energy to devote to the present. An important recommendation, though: *make sure you keep this letter private;* dispose of it completely once you're finished with it.

Volunteer to Help Others

Finally, you can honor your loved one's memory by helping others. Doing so can take any of several different forms. You can volunteer for a cause that your loved one supported. If he or she died of a specific illness, you can raise money or donate time to a foundation dedicated to curing that disease. You can also help support a cause that's completely unrelated—a cause that's worthwhile to support and that will "get you out of the house" and focusing on something beyond your own grief. Any of these efforts can be a great way to memorialize your loved one. One suggestion, though: don't take these steps until you're truly ready, as you'll want to have sufficient energy and clarity of mind to take on the task.

All of the suggestions in this chapter are just that—suggestions. You're the only person who can decide what's likely to work for you, so I'm not saying that anything I've mentioned here is the best bet for helping you deal with grief. Perhaps you'll find these ideas useful; perhaps not. See what you think. Take what's useful and ignore the rest.

Something I strongly urge you to do, however, is *not* to keep your grief all to yourself. It's important to share your feelings with someone you trust. It's important to find a person who can help you work through the grief process without feeling so alone.

That's the subject I'd like to raise next.

NOTES

1. Virginia A. Simpson, private e-mail correspondence.
2. See www.quotationspage.com.
3. See www.quotationspage.com.
4. See www.quotationspage.com.

6

More Things That Help

I hope that the suggestions in the previous chapter help you ease the burden of grief. Here are some additional ideas that can make a difference as you cope with your loss.

CONFIDE IN OTHERS

One of the most important things you can do during bereavement is let someone close to you know what you're feeling. Grief isn't something you should face alone. You need to share your emotions as the grief process unfolds. If you have a supportive, trustworthy person to confide in, you'll

> Grief is best facilitated when teens are able to show their emotional pain, talk with others, express their feelings about the death, and accept support from family and friends.
> —Marty Tousley, Hospice of the Valley, Phoenix, Arizona[1]

have a much easier time—less painful and more comfortable—as you recover from grief. But the key words here are *supportive* and *trustworthy*. I can't emphasize strongly enough how crucial it is that this person be someone who has your best interests in mind.

A Parent or Other Relative . . .

The person or persons you confide in may be one or both of your parents. It may be a brother, a sister, or perhaps an aunt or uncle. It may be a grandparent. What's most important is that

you choose someone whom you can trust and who will listen to
you without judging your words or feelings.

Keep in mind that the people you're closest to may be
struggling with their own experiences of grief. Let's say that
your father has died. Your mother will probably be trying hard
to be supportive of
you, but at the same
time she'll be
struggling with her
own emotions over
losing her husband,
which may
complicate her
effort to help you.

It takes a while to get over death. I was left alone a lot after
my grandfather's death so that was twice as hard on me. Stay
[together] as a family after such a big loss—it helps.
—**Dana, late teens**

My aunt also helped me cope with the loss.

—**Aundrea, thirteen**

The same would be true for a brother or sister, who would feel
bereaved in ways that are similar to what you're feeling. For
this reason, sometimes it's best to find support from a person
who isn't coping with grief as intense as yours.

Your Friends . . .

If your friends are supportive, you might be able to confide in them about what you're feeling. Friends can be a wonderful source of emotional support during bereavement. But keep in mind that despite their good intentions, some people may not be able to understand what you're going through. They may not have experienced any losses themselves, or they may find your situation confusing or threatening. Their reactions *don't* mean that there's anything wrong with you. They may "pull back" emotionally, however, because they're not sure what to do or say. On the other hand, some friends can be great sources of strength during difficult times.

Grieving teens do best when they're helped to find peers who've also experienced a death. They're often very relieved to discover they're not the only ones who've had someone close to them die.

—Marty Tousley[2]

Your Teacher or Counselor . . .

Another possibility is to talk with a teacher or school counselor about what you're going through. If you're close to one of the adults at your school, consider seeking out him or her for emotional support. Some of them may even have had specific training to help teenagers deal with personal crises, including loss of loved ones. In any case, it's important for your teachers to know what you're going through, since they can then take your personal circumstances into account within the school setting.

A Member of the Clergy . . .

If you attend a church, temple, mosque, or other place of worship, you may be able to find support from someone among the clergy. Many members of the clergy make themselves available to reassure and support their congregations. Some have training in pastoral counseling. As in the other situations we've discussed, be sure that you're comfortable with the clergyperson you've selected to confide in.

Teens on talking about grief:

Talk about them [the person who died]. Although it seems hard to talk at first, it's better.

—Dana, late teens

Spending time with my friends was the best thing. Being with family it seemed like they had to be serious, because they were grieving too. But when I was with friends they weren't afraid to make me laugh.

—Nikki, mid-teens

My five best friends were my true help, even though I only knew one of them at the time of my father's death. Three of them came to my grandmother's wake. Three came to the funeral mass. It's really nice to know that you have friends to comfort you.

—Janice, eighteen

My friends all knew I was there, but they didn't understand it, I was ruining their fun. The only one that talked to me was one of my brothers friends. Him and my bro were so close, he cried with me as the new year came in.

—Louisa, college age

SEEK HELP FROM A PSYCHOTHERAPIST OR COUNSELOR

Most people benefit from having a guide to help them understand their personal and family past. A trained psychotherapist or counselor can ask you questions, help you see patterns, and clarify

The first person I called after my mom died was my JROTC instructor. He called my other instructors and they ordered flowers for the funeral. It was the biggest arrangement of flowers there. Then they got five of my friends together and brought them to my moms viewing. My *friends* had to be the most important people at the time. My best friend was there for me the most. She lost her father a year before my mom died. So she knew what I was going through which really helped.

—Nikki, mid-teens

events that occurred during your childhood or are occurring now. In the midst of family life, it may be difficult for you to make those

Teenagers crave normalcy of what their life was like prior to a death, divorce, etc. Teenagers *need* to talk about whatever has happened, but on their terms and with people of their choosing.

—Sarah, fifteen

connections precisely because the task is fraught with emotions; it's hard to be objective from such a close perspective. A skilled therapist, however, can help facilitate insights partly because of his

Bereavement is a normal experience and most people grieve with their friends and family. If these usual supports are not helping or the grief is causing extreme impairment in everyday functioning, or going on intensely for longer than expected, or for young people who are vulnerable then they may benefit from more formal help.

—Dr. Ann York, Child and Family Consultation Centre, London, England[3]

or her greater objectivity. In addition, a therapist can reassure you about difficult aspects of this task that may be confusing or upsetting as you encounter them.

Psychotherapy can also offer another advantage: a second chance at being "parented" by someone who is consistent, nonjudgmental, and possibly more understanding than your own parents have been. Individual therapists' skills vary; however, a good psychotherapist can provide you with the chance to perceive your life in new ways. This situation can be especially helpful at a time of personal crisis.

Some people, including teens, feel reluctant to seek counseling or therapy during bereavement. They may worry that seeing a counselor means that "something is wrong" with them, or that only "crazy people" see a psychotherapist. However, there's nothing wrong with getting professional help, and doing so doesn't mean you're crazy. Many people seek therapists' guidance for family conflicts, job problems, and all sorts of other crises, so why shouldn't grief receive the same concern? There's no reason to face this task alone. Talking with a trained counselor or therapist can make the grief process smoother, easier, and a lot less lonely.

The Nature of Therapy

What's therapy like during bereavement? It's such a personal experience that I'm not sure if anyone's experience is *typical*. But many people who enter therapy following a major loss often do so to seek help for one or more of the following issues.

Emotional Issues

Many people feel depressed, lonely, angry, guilty, and confused in the aftermath of a major loss. These are normal emotions, but their intensity sometimes exceeds what people find comfortable or even tolerable. Psychotherapy can help you deal with these complex emotions.

Physical Issues

If your grief includes sleep disturbances, eating problems, severe fatigue, or other health-related issues, a therapist can assist you in coping with your difficulties.

Family Issues

Conflicts between family members following a tragedy aren't uncommon. Rather than trying to make sense of them alone, however, you may find that a psychotherapist can help you solve problems and ease tensions.

Existential Issues

Death and grief frequently reveal new meanings to our lives, or else cast old meanings into doubt. In the aftermath of a loved one's death, you may start to wonder what went on in your past, or you may wish to change your behavior in the future. Therapy can help you understand these *existential* issues—the issues that concern the meaning of existence.

> If you are hurting, cry. If you are angry, scream. You may look stupid but it helps. Talking to people is *very* helpful as well.
> —Marcie, late teens

There may be other reasons for seeking therapy, but most people who do so during bereavement are dealing with at least one of these issues, and often with more than one. Simply determining where one issue leaves off and another starts may be difficult. Such complicated aspects of our feelings can become entangled. Following a loved one's death, for instance, most people feel depressed—but what causes the depression? Is it a sense of loss? Loneliness? Is it perhaps a side effect of unexpressed anger? What are the results of all these emotions? What's most important is to stay open to what you're feeling, and to seek guidance if you feel a need for it.

Kinds of Therapy

Therapists use many different techniques. In general, therapy during the grief process serves much the same purposes as it does under other circumstances. It allows you to express emotions. It provides a place for clarifying problems and exploring possible solutions. It encourages careful decision making. Also, it builds confidence between you and the therapist in ways that help you to undertake

> I saw a counselor after my mom died because I felt depressed and also wasn't getting along with my brothers. I thought therapy would be a waste of time, but I worked through a lot of things and felt less depressed than I did before. I also realized that my arguments with my brothers were partly a result of our all being upset about Mom's death.
> —Stan, nineteen

these other tasks together. Early on, therapy may focus on the bewilderment, anger, and depression that you feel right after a parent's death. Later, it may shift to examine other matters—what took place in the past or what's going to happen in the future.

One-to-One Therapy

Therapists have many methods for helping people deal with bereavement. Here are some comments by William K. Dixon, a psychotherapist in Denver, Colorado, about how he works with bereaved patients in one-to-one therapy.

What I often invite people to do when they want some help working through grief is to imagine, if they're willing, the person they have lost. Sometimes it's helpful to do that even as if at the funeral or at the deathbed. For some people, it's more helpful to imagine a time shortly before death, so that they can have that sense of expressing something to the person while that person would still have been able to listen.

What I ask them to do, then, is to begin expressing some things with that person: some things which they particularly appreciate; some things which they feel bad about; some things which made them feel fortunate; and even some things which make them resentful. People often feel that when someone dies, they have no right to be angry with the person; they think they're required to forgive everything. But a lot of times, that forgiveness can't happen until the person gets in touch with the resentments which have lingered. And so I try to find an opportunity for the person to express those resentments as directly as possible.

Something else which also seems to be helpful is asking the client to imagine what they are taking with them from that relationship. It might be particular memories; it might be a skill that they learned from that person; it might be a certain attitude or feeling which they want to continue to have. Conversely, I ask them what they want to leave behind or bury with that person. Sometimes that's where some of the forgiveness happens. "I'm leaving behind those memories of painful times we had," for instance. Or, "I'm leaving behind the resentment I feel for the times you scolded me." And they express that.

103

Finally, I ask the person to say good-bye. Often, a person is
not really willing to say good-bye. Certainly a person can say
those words; but in terms of being able to say good-bye and
leave the person behind—so that they have psychologically
buried the one they've lost—that may be another matter. If they
resist that, then I acknowledge it. And I check with them if that
might be an indication that some feelings are left unexpressed,
and that psychologically this is the reason why it's hard to let go.
Generally, people are able to recognize that there's still some
unfinished business. There are some strong feelings. And it's too
soon to really imagine letting go. In that case, we generally agree
to come back to that. It usually seems appropriate to the client.

This process might take place over one session that we'll use for this purpose, or it might take place over a period of several months. There is a lot of individual difference, of course. Sometimes I encourage a person to deal with just part of the grief. At a later time, when the person seems to be readier, then we can proceed. People generally have a good sense of their own timing.[5]

Bereavement Groups

One alternative to individual therapy is the *bereavement group*. (Organizers and members also call them "grief workshops," "bereavement seminars," "mourning clinics," and so forth.) These groups all provide some form of group therapy. Some stress self-help and are a form of peer counseling. Others use a trained *facilitator*— sometimes a volunteer, sometimes a paid staff member—to provide guidance in ways that might otherwise be lacking. Either way, the members meet to discuss their

> I also recommend finding a group where they can share their experiences with others so that they will come to know that their thoughts and feelings are normal. And if they don't want a group, to find an experienced grief counselor. They need to understand that being strong means knowing when to reach out to others, not holding everything inside.
> —Virginia A. Simpson, Ph.D., executive director, Mourning Star Center, Palm Desert, California[6]

problems; they listen to each other and perhaps offer suggestions or encouragement; however, they do not necessarily perform therapy in a traditional sense. The emphasis most often is on mutual supportiveness among people facing similar predicaments.

Omega, a bereavement support agency located in Somerville, Massachusetts, near Boston, offers emotional support and information for the ill, the dying, their families, and the bereaved. Omega provides several distinct services, including bereavement groups. Evelyn Gladu, a psychotherapist and grief counselor who is Omega's former director, explains how this organization helps its clients: "All we do is to create a safe place for people to express whatever they feel during their grief.

Different people use the group in different ways. We set it up so that people can respond in a way that will be helpful to them."[7]

What happens to people during an Omega group? The bereavement group provides a "safe place" in which members of the group can feel and express what may have seemed embarrassing or even forbidden elsewhere. Crying, laughter, anger, and expressions of other emotions are all permissible. This in itself frequently allows participants an intense feeling of relief. There is also a social dimension to the experience. Group members each discover that the others have gone through experiences similar to their own, that at least *some* people understand what bereavement is like. This affirms the participants' sense that their emotions are not only normal but perhaps even necessary for getting through a difficult phase of life. Ms. Gladu suggests that the result of these insights on the group and its members is often a stronger, more confident grasp of the meaning of loss.

What Therapy Does

Psychotherapy is a deeply personal, individual experience, so it's hard—perhaps impossible—to summarize what happens when a therapist and a patient work together. Some people find that therapy serves mostly as a "safety valve" for releasing intense emotions. Others feel that therapy helps them accept their loss. Others benefit from the ability of therapy to clarify events in the past. Still others use therapy as a way to solve problems in the present. Psychotherapy isn't any one thing; it's an opportunity to explore the issues you're facing and make sense of them in keeping with what *you* need.

Grief is only the beginning.

> **Here are some comments that teens have made about their experiences with therapy:**
>
> **My therapist was a rock—the most reliable thing in my life.**
> **—Winnie, eighteen**
>
> **Therapy helped me cope with what happened after Mom died.**
> **—Carlo, sixteen**
>
> **Therapy helped me understand my behavior and take risks for change.**
> **—Sari, seventeen**
>
> **My counselor helped me separate my anger, fear, and grief—to try to cope with them one at a time.**
> **—Janine, sixteen**

FIND WEB-BASED RESOURCES

In recent years, the web has started to offer a new alternative for the bereaved. Certain websites provide resources about grief—information about the grief process and, in some cases, message boards in which you can share your experiences with other bereaved teens. For instance, Beyondindigo.com offers on-line articles about various aspects of the grief process plus resources specifically intended for teenagers. Goodgrief.org offers similar resources. Griefhealing.com has information of these sorts as well as message boards specifically intended for people who wish to share their thoughts following a major loss.

These and other sites have the potential for being useful to bereaved teenagers. If you seek information from websites,

however, you should take the same precautions as when visiting any other sites:

- ◎ **Don't identify yourself by any means other than your screen name**
- ◎ **Don't provide any identifying information (phone number, address, and so forth)**
- ◎ **Don't assume that the other people using message boards, chat rooms, and so forth, are who they claim or seem to be**
- ◎ **If you have any concerns about your on-line safety, alert your parents to the situation immediately.**

In addition, you shouldn't use the web as a substitute for face-to-face interactions with someone who knows you well and genuinely cares for you. Web-based resources can be informative and helpful, but they can't provide the same support, insight, and compassion as interacting with a thoughtful, compassionate human being.

Grief is not graceful.

—Mariette Hartley, American actress[8]

Chapter 9 of this book, "Resources," includes a list of websites that may provide worthwhile information.

READ BOOKS ABOUT GRIEF AND BEREAVEMENT

Finally, consider an old standby: books. Hundreds of good books about loss and bereavement are available, including many intended specifically for a teenage audience. Chapter 9 includes a useful sampling. Again, reading books isn't a substitute for talking about your grief with someone you trust, but learning about bereavement can help you make sense of what's happened and move on with your life.

NOTES

1. Marty Tousley, private e-mail correspondence.
2. Marty Tousley, private e-mail correspondence.
3. Ann York, private e-mail correspondence.
4. See www.quotationspage.com.
5. William K. Dixon, private interview.
6. Virginia A. Simpson, private e-mail correspondence.
7. Evelyn Gladu, private interview.
8. See www.quotationspage.com.

7 Warning Signs

Bereavement is hard, but most people cope successfully with this stressful experience, come to terms with loss, and adapt to life without the person they loved. The likelihood is that you will too.

But what if you have a more problematic time during bereavement? What if you have more difficulty getting on with your life? Sometimes the normal process breaks down. Bereavement experts call this "troubled (or complicated) grief." This isn't common, but it happens for some people. If it happens to you, how should you deal with it?

There's no simple answer to that question. However, certain warning signs exist. Here's an overview of the warning signs, what they mean, and what you can do about them.

> There are many factors that can influence the course and outcome of an individual teen's adjustment to loss. Nevertheless, because it is a time of such great change, with all the losses attached to those changes, adolescence can be one of the most difficult and confusing stages of life. Teens want very much to be independent from the rest of us, but they still need the caring, the presence and the support of the adults in their lives.
>
> —Marty Tousley,
> Hospice of the Valley,
> Phoenix, Arizona[1]

WARNING SIGN 1

Prolonged Inability to Believe That the Death Has Truly Occurred

In chapter 2, I described how shock and disbelief are a common early reaction to the death of someone you love. It's hard to imagine that the person you've lost is really gone. It's hard to

believe that the loss is permanent. The resulting shock is a
normal reaction to loss, so don't be surprised if you have this
reaction early on. If this sense of disbelief continues for a long
time, however—if you just can't accept your loss despite the
passage of many weeks or months—then what you're feeling
may be a sign of troubled grief.

This kind of denial should prompt you to seek help. The first
step is probably to speak with your parents about what you're
feeling. If the loss you've suffered is a parent's death, talk to the
other parent. If that's not advisable (such as when your
surviving parent is too severely bereaved to respond to your
grief), then I suggest raising the issue with a trusted
grandparent, aunt, or uncle. Other possibilities include a
trusted teacher, a school counselor, or a member of the clergy.
One way or another, I strongly recommend that you find help
from an adult who can assist you in coping with your grief.
What's most important is to select someone who can be
supportive and then to confide in that person about what
you're feeling. (Throughout this chapter I stress the importance
of interacting *with people you truly trust*. This is crucial
anyway, but especially during the grief process, which is why I
mention it over and over.)

WARNING SIGN 2

Prolonged Depression

In chapter 2, I mentioned that sadness and depression, like shock and disbelief, are a normal early experience during bereavement. When someone you love dies, you have good reason to feel sad. Even depression—which is a more complex and potentially serious emotional state than sadness—is an understandable reaction to severe loss. But if your sadness or depression

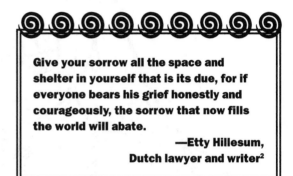

Give your sorrow all the space and shelter in yourself that is its due, for if everyone bears his grief honestly and courageously, the sorrow that now fills the world will abate.

—Etty Hillesum,
Dutch lawyer and writer[2]

Warning Signs of Depression:

- Intense or prolonged unhappiness
- Withdrawal into apathy and helplessness
- Feelings of worthlessness, hopelessness, and helplessness
- Increase in irritability or restlessness
- Retreating into isolation
- Significant drop in academic performance
- Decline or loss of interest in activities that used to be sources of enjoyment
- Intense or prolonged fatigue or lack of energy or motivation
- Self-neglect or self-damaging behavior (such as cutting)
- Preoccupation with sad thoughts or death
- Intense or prolonged loss of concentration
- Sudden or frequent outbursts of temper
- Reckless or dangerous behavior
- Increase in physical complaints
- Major change in sleep habits
- Major change in eating habits
- Drug or alcohol abuse.

continue for a long time, it's crucial that you speak with someone about what you're feeling. Perhaps there's no reason to be concerned; however, it's a good idea to check. You don't want to suffer unnecessarily.

How long is too long? That's a difficult question to answer. Depression following a major loss can go on for months or longer. Even if your depression is understandable, given the magnitude of your loss, there's no reason for you to "slug it out" alone. Talking with a trusted adult can be a useful first step in working your way out of depression. Many teens benefit from a trained counselor's help, perhaps by speaking with a psychologist, social worker, or psychiatrist. There's nothing wrong with seeking assistance of these sorts. On the contrary, finding a "guide" during bereavement can be a huge boost in regaining your balance following a loss. (See chapter 6 for descriptions of different kinds of grief counseling and psychotherapy.)

WARNING SIGN 3

Prolonged Feelings of Severe Stress

Like everyone else, teens find even normal day-to-day life full of hassles. It's not surprising that dealing with grief *in addition* to life's ordinary challenges increases your stress level. Bereavement often includes feelings of internal stresses (anxiety, confusion, worries about the future) as well as external stresses (money issues, family conflicts, social pressures). Here again the issue isn't *whether* you're feeling stressed but rather *how much* and for *how long*. If you feel stressed by either the normal demands on your time and attention, the unusual demands of bereavement, or both, I recommend that you seek help from a trusted adult. Explaining what you're feeling is a good first step in dealing with the situation. In addition, consider taking some specific steps to ease the stress you feel.

My own grief was a boulder that I carried everywhere.

—Margaret Todd Maitland, American writer and editor[3]

Consider rereading chapters 5 and 6 in this book, which offer a wide variety of methods that can help relieve stress. In

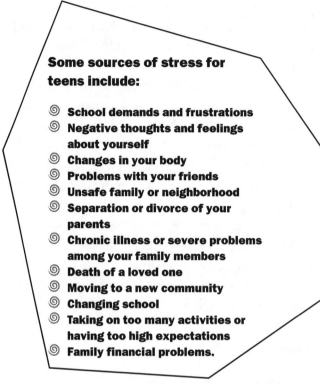

Some sources of stress for teens include:

- ◎ School demands and frustrations
- ◎ Negative thoughts and feelings about yourself
- ◎ Changes in your body
- ◎ Problems with your friends
- ◎ Unsafe family or neighborhood
- ◎ Separation or divorce of your parents
- ◎ Chronic illness or severe problems among your family members
- ◎ Death of a loved one
- ◎ Moving to a new community
- ◎ Changing school
- ◎ Taking on too many activities or having too high expectations
- ◎ Family financial problems.

addition, working with a therapist or counselor may provide other useful methods.

WARNING SIGN 4

Inability to Care for Yourself

For a few people grief can become so severe that the bereaved person loses the ability to care for himself or herself. This situation isn't common. It's not out of the question, however, that you may become so fatigued or depressed following a major loss that you become emotionally disorganized and unable to perform your normal obligations. A small number of people struggle to cope with daily life during bereavement. If you're having this kind of difficulty—if you're so depressed that you can't get out of bed, can't eat, or can't function at school or at home—you should seek adult help immediately.

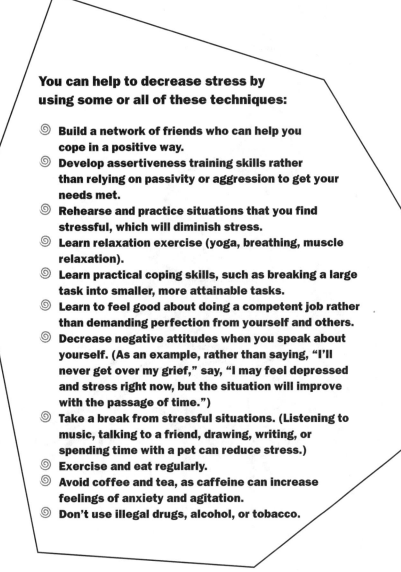

You can help to decrease stress by using some or all of these techniques:

- ⊚ Build a network of friends who can help you cope in a positive way.
- ⊚ Develop assertiveness training skills rather than relying on passivity or aggression to get your needs met.
- ⊚ Rehearse and practice situations that you find stressful, which will diminish stress.
- ⊚ Learn relaxation exercise (yoga, breathing, muscle relaxation).
- ⊚ Learn practical coping skills, such as breaking a large task into smaller, more attainable tasks.
- ⊚ Learn to feel good about doing a competent job rather than demanding perfection from yourself and others.
- ⊚ Decrease negative attitudes when you speak about yourself. (As an example, rather than saying, "I'll never get over my grief," say, "I may feel depressed and stress right now, but the situation will improve with the passage of time.")
- ⊚ Take a break from stressful situations. (Listening to music, talking to a friend, drawing, writing, or spending time with a pet can reduce stress.)
- ⊚ Exercise and eat regularly.
- ⊚ Avoid coffee and tea, as caffeine can increase feelings of anxiety and agitation.
- ⊚ Don't use illegal drugs, alcohol, or tobacco.

For a while I felt so bad I wanted to curl up and not do anything at all, ever.

—Leslie, fifteen

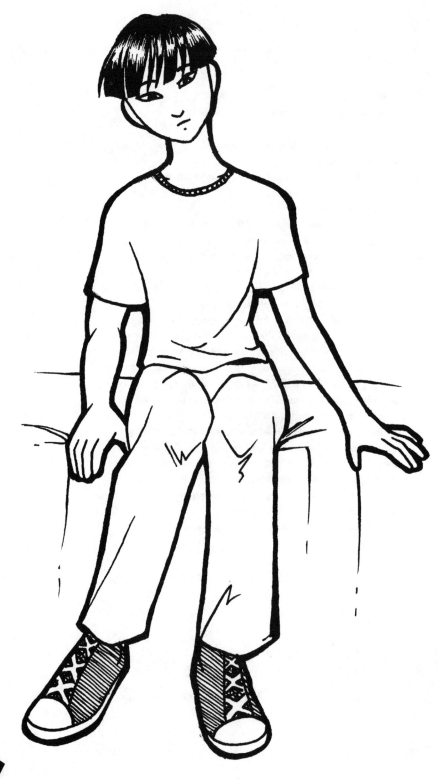

WARNING SIGN 5

Inability to "Get On with Life," to Reconnect with the World, or to Invest Energy in Living

Perhaps you can manage your daily tasks, such as going to school and interacting with your family and friends, but you feel disconnected from life or indifferent about people and activities that used to mean much to you. This reaction, like others we've discussed, is a common response during the early phases of grief. Many people feel a need to pull back from the outside world right after a major loss. You may end up withdrawing for a while to protect yourself, conserve energy, and heal your emotional injuries. There's nothing wrong with that approach in the early phases of bereavement. After a while, though, it's important to reconnect with the world. If you find that you *can't* reconnect, it's time to get assistance.

Ways to "jump-start" yourself during bereavement:

- Do something you enjoy—listen to music, play a sport, eat out at a favorite restaurant
- Make contact with someone who's important to you—a friend, a relative, an adult you trust and like
- Express yourself in a letter or journal, or on tape or video, to get your feelings out
- Get outside and *move*
- Find a therapist or grief counselor to confide in
- Join a bereavement support group
- Volunteer to help someone.

See chapters 5 and 6 for other ideas that may be useful in moving onward.

Another warning sign is prolonged social isolation. Again, it's understandable that following your loss, you may need to spend more time than usual by yourself—that's not a problem. Grief is one of those experiences where it's appropriate, even creative, to pull inward to some degree and seek more solitude than usual. Solitude can be a wonderful solace during bereavement. Time alone is a way of conserving energy, thinking through what has happened, and replenishing your emotional resources.

However, the *degree* and *duration* of your solitude is significant. If you refuse all or most contact with other human beings, or if your isolation goes on and on, then I urge you to seek help. Prolonged isolation can indicate problematic bereavement. The best response is to reach out to someone you trust, explain what you're feeling, and seek help in connecting with the wider world.

> During Mom's illness I felt so tired I didn't really have the energy to be with anyone. I just wanted to be alone. This got to be a habit—I ignored everybody and after a while they ignored me back. Then Mom died and by then I'd kind of alienated people already, so I was on my own. They were sympathetic but didn't want much to do with me. I didn't make it easy for them. So I kept to myself, kind of like a wounded animal hiding in the woods. I now realize that wasn't good and made things more difficult.
>
> —Ryan, seventeen

WARNING SIGN 6

Thinking Too Much about the Loss

Some people find that during bereavement, they can't stop thinking about the loss they've suffered. They obsess about the person who died. They feel haunted by scenes of that person's illness or accident. In some cases, they struggle with feelings of responsibility—an unrealistic belief that they were somehow responsible for what happened or that they should have somehow prevented the tragedy from occurring. These feelings and memory "flashbacks" are common and normal early on during the grief process, and you shouldn't worry about them at that stage. But if they linger a long time, or if you can't sleep or concentrate because of these preoccupations, it's worthwhile to explain what you're feeling to a trained counselor or therapist.

> Even though I knew Tad [Lukas's brother] was dead, I keep thinking I'm seeing him. I see a guy walking in the hallway at school and for a second I think it's Tad. I'm in a store and I hear someone talking and it sounds so much like Tad's voice that I turn and expect to see him, but he's not there. This sort of thing's happening over and over. Sometimes I think I'm going crazy. I just can't get him out of my head.
>
> —Lukas, seventeen

Similarly, working hard to *avoid* thinking about your loss can indicate a problem. Most people find that with the passage of time, they think less frequently, and with less intensity, about the person who died. This process occurs on its own. It may take months to occur, but it's self-sustaining. If you have to struggle to take your mind off your grief, or if you feel burdened by the effort, you're better off if you find a trusted adult who will listen to what you're feeling.

WARNING SIGN 7

Substantial Weight Gain, Substantial Weight Loss, or Marked Deterioration of Health

There's no doubt that grief affects your body as well as your mind. During bereavement, most people feel less energetic, and many feel burdened or "dragged down" by the heavy moods they experience. Many experience shifts in their appetite—perhaps a lack of interest in food. In addition, some feel

unhealthy or unfit as they cope with the intense emotions of grief. These are all understandable reactions. Are they a problem? Not necessarily.

However, intense or prolonged disruptions of your physical well-being may be warning signs of troubled grief. If you find that you're heavily overeating, for instance, that may indicate a problem. The same holds true for a protracted lack of interest in food. Gaining or losing significant amounts of weight can tip you off that you're struggling to regain your emotional balance during bereavement. Similarly, a deterioration of your health—a lot of colds, stomach bugs, headaches, or other symptoms—can signal difficulties during the grief process.

> When I'm under stress I overeat. Martha's [her sister's] death was the worst thing I ever went through, and that was definitely stressful, and I definitely overate as part of how I responded to that.
>
> —Jane, late teens

My recommendations: first, reread chapters 5 and 6 about ways in which you can help yourself at this difficult time. If the suggestions there don't help, raise the issue of your health with your parents or some other trusted adult. A physical exam may be a good idea. You're probably fine, but having the doctor identify any problems (or give you a clean bill of health) can be a great boost to your mind as well as your body.

WARNING SIGN 8

Reliance on Alcohol or Drugs to Relieve Your Anguish, Loneliness, Anger, or Other Emotions

Bereavement can alter your daily routines, sleep patterns, appetite, and emotions. Grief is also stressful in its own right. As a result, you may feel a need to ease the pressure by resorting to alcohol or drugs. This is a bad idea in several ways. First of all, there are many risks associated with alcohol and drug use. In addition, drinking alcohol or taking drugs to ease your grief can complicate your bereavement rather than simplify it. One reason is that you may become more reliant on drinking or drug-taking than you would be at other times. Another reason is that alcohol and drug abuse won't help you cope with bereavement; they will just disrupt and postpone the tasks you face.

> There was lots of drinking at the wake for my dad. That's part of what happens at a wake. Drinking was how my relatives coped with the situation. What was hard was that I wanted to join them but couldn't, so I'd go drink with my friends later. For a while I was really screwed up.
> —Derek, seventeen

If you feel that you're abusing alcohol or drugs during bereavement, you should consult a qualified counselor for advice. Drugs and alcohol can't lead you through the grief process. They will only obstruct your way back to a normal life. Chapter 9, "Resources," includes information about finding help to deal with alcohol and drug abuse.

WARNING SIGN 9

Suicidal Thoughts or Gestures, or Attempted Suicide

Grief can be so painful that it's hard to imagine when the pain will end or how you'll survive it till it's over. It may be tempting to fantasize that your death is the answer to this problem. But that's not true. Grief *is* painful, and nothing simple or quick will take the pain away. Bereavement is difficult and seems to last forever. Yet killing yourself makes no sense. As the saying goes, "suicide is a permanent solution to a temporary problem."

It's true that some people, including teenagers, have suicidal thoughts during the grief process. For many teens, these thoughts take shape in passive ways, such as just wishing that they'd never wake up. For a few, it means self-destructive gestures, such as self-cutting.

If you feel you're in immediate danger of killing yourself, tell someone you trust right away or dial 911 and explain the situation. Or else call the National Suicide Hotline at 1-800-SUICIDE.

In addition to alerting a responsible, caring adult to what you feel, I suggest that you take these additional actions:

- *Avoid alcohol and drugs*, which can aggravate depression, complicate clear thinking, and prolong the grief process.
- *Try to problem-solve.* If you feel burdened by the tasks you have to face, break your responsibilities down, take the first things first, and pace yourself on the rest.
- *Live life one day at a time.* Don't try to figure out everything all at once. Although life may seem hopelessly complicated, you'll cope with everything sooner or later. This is true for grief as well as for the rest; you'll feel better little by little.
- *Think about your family and friends.* You probably underestimate the value that your life has to other people, and you can't imagine how devastating your death will be to them.
- *Try to believe that no matter how bad you feel now, you will feel better in the future!*

If you have these thoughts or do any of these acts, talk to a trusted adult as soon as possible. Don't hide your feelings and just wish they'd go away. Find help fast.

If you're taking any direct steps toward suicide, find help immediately. Talk to your parents, your teacher, your counselor, relatives or family friends. Holding your emotions in won't help—it's crucial for someone you trust to know what you're feeling.

Here are other issues that should prompt you to seek help:

- If you have a history of suicidal thoughts or gestures—driving recklessly on purpose, taking overdoses, or threatening to kill yourself
- If you spend a lot of time thinking about death or planning to die
- If you're "putting your affairs in order"—giving away possessions, planning your funeral, or saying good-bye to friends as if for the last time
- If you have a history of clinical depression.

If you feel that you are experiencing problems in any of these ways, you should contact a qualified counselor for help. What you are going through is probably not a long-term problem, but you will be better off discussing the issues than ignoring them.

TAKING THE LONG VIEW

One of the hardest things about the grief process is that when you're in the middle of it, you find it difficult to believe that you'll ever find your way out. You struggle to imagine that you'll feel better again someday. You worry that you'll feel angry, depressed, and lonely forever.

The truth is that grief eases with the passage of time. Although nothing will make your pain magically disappear, you'll gradually adjust to your loss and come to terms with it. You'll eventually regain a normal sense of life. You'll remember how to enjoy activities, friends, and yourself again.

The key: take the long view. Don't expect healing to happen all at once—and don't go it alone.

NOTES

1. Marty Tousley, private e-mail correspondence.
2. See www.quotationspage.com.
3. See www.quotationspage.com.

Conclusion

As much as I'd like to, I can't tidy up our discussion and wrap it neatly in a bow. The nature of bereavement is to be uncertain and unresolved. At the same time, I'd like to conclude this book with a few final summaries, observations, and reflections.

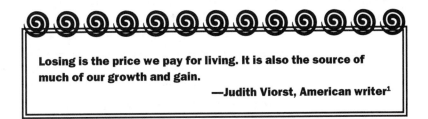

Losing is the price we pay for living. It is also the source of much of our growth and gain.

—Judith Viorst, American writer[1]

GRIEF IS NORMAL

I've said this earlier, but I need to say it again: grief is normal. If you love someone, your loss of that person will hit you hard. The resulting grief is painful, but the pain doesn't mean that what you're going through is abnormal. On the contrary, pain is an inevitable part of grief. You will endure the pain and, sooner or later, return to a more stable sense of things.

However, grief may feel strange precisely because of its intense and often unpredictable feelings. Many people—teenagers as well as others—feel "out of control" during bereavement. The sadness, anger, frustration, anguish, and confusion feel chaotic and even dangerous during much of the grief process. Rest assured that even that sensation of being out of control is usually part of what happens. It's important for you to let yourself feel what you're feeling. The key: express your emotions in a safe place, ideally with an adult who you can trust to accept your feelings without judgment. Accepting the reality of your grief—as well as the reality of loss—will help you cope with the new reality you face.

YOUR EXPERIENCE IS UNIQUE

Although the grief process may include fairly predictable emotions and follow a fairly predictable sequence of phases, you will experience bereavement in your own individual way. No one else had the relationship you had with your loved one, and no one will feel the loss precisely as you do.

> Sometimes it tickles your toes other times it knocks you down. Just because I feel this way doesn't mean you will. Because I have to do this doesn't mean you have to.
> —Louisa, college age

For these reasons, what you feel, how you express your feelings, and how long this experience goes on, are all unique to your own personality and circumstances. You may end up falling silent when others might cry or shout, or you may feel overwhelmed with emotion when others might withdraw into silence. Your grief may last

How you grieve will depend on many circumstances, including:

- Your age
- Your stage of emotional development
- Your personality
- Your involvement with the process of looking after the person who died (in the case of illness)
- Your prior experiences with death
- Whether the deceased person died suddenly or over a longer period of time
- Your social support systems (family, friends and/or community).

longer than other people's grief, or for a shorter period of time. It's important for you to "go with the flow" and not tell yourself what you should or shouldn't be feeling.

BEREAVEMENT ISN'T ABOUT "RIGHT" OR "WRONG"

Each culture has its own customs about mourning and grief. Some encourage emotional expressiveness; some expect a more self-contained response. Many involve elaborate rituals; others emphasize more individualized expression. For instance, many Jews observe a ritual called *sitting shiva*—"a seven-day period of withdrawal from the world," according to American writer Anita Diamant—which is "intended to foster the difficult but healing work of grief."[3] Catholics and other Christians may hold a *wake,* an occasion during which mourners gather to talk, pray, and sing, as well as memorialize the deceased person in other ways. Protestants of many denominations have mourning customs that focus on funeral services composed of prayers, remembrances of the person who died, and hymns or other forms of music. Members of the Society of Friends (the Quakers) often hold memorial services in which any member of the community can speak spontaneously about the person who died.

Similarly, Muslim mourning customs include *wahshat* and *'Isha* prayers, which, in accordance with the Qur'an, console the living as well as marking the deceased person's death. Islam also prescribes specific burial practices.

Hindu and Buddhist mourning customs vary greatly throughout the world. In Nepal and India, for instance, family members witness or take part in rituals performed by priests, who chant, pray, and burn incense on behalf of the deceased. Buddhists also perform rites that serve to ease the dead person's departure from this life and simultaneously help the family and community adjust to their loss.

Your own ethnic or religious background may involve specific observances following a death among your family members or friends. However, it's important to realize that although communities may stress particular sorts of rituals and customs, there's no "right" or "wrong" way to experience the loss you've suffered. You have a right to feel what you're feeling.

GRIEF ISN'T QUICKLY "OVER AND DONE WITH"

Following a loss, almost everyone wants to know when his or her bereavement will end. The truth is that grief never really stops; instead, it changes and diminishes. You *will* feel better! But the journey of accepting your loss is unpredictable, and part of the reality of grief is that it tapers off rather than stopping completely. If you have loved someone deeply, you can adjust to his or her absence from your life, but you never really forget that person or lose a sense of how important he or she was to you.

You may have heard people refer to "closure" following a loss—a sense of closing a door, perhaps, on the pain of grief. They'll say things like, "We're looking for closure after this tragedy." This concept is understandable; we all want bereavement to be done. But it's a misleading concept too, because grief is so complex, so personal, and so powerful that in

> This is the third year since my mom's death. I am still sad a lot knowing my mom won't be there for me in person. But she will be there in spirit. When I am alone at night, it is usually when it hits me. I cry and sometimes it really hurts but I think it is as important to cry as it is to laugh.
>
> —Nikki, mid-teens

I truly *hate* people who say "the pain will go away." It *never* does. But day by day it lessens until the pain is overcome by the happy memories, and you can go on with life knowing that even though you still hurt, life goes on, and your loved one would be proud of you, and is proud of you, and is there. Living life for yourself and your loved one, being a living memorial for them, moving on but never *ever* forgetting—this is possible and something to look forward to for tomorrow. That is the best way for me, and I hope others.
                                            —Janice, eighteen

many ways you never really put it behind you like a closed door. I suggest this approach instead.

First, rest assured that the acute pain of grief will diminish with the passage of time.

Second, take the time you need. You can't rush bereavement; just let it happen.

Third, feel confident that you'll regain your emotional balance and return to the full richness of life. I know it's hard to believe that now, but it's true.

A FEW LAST THOUGHTS FROM THE EXPERTS . . .

Here are what some experts who work with teenagers say about bereavement:

I believe grief is a life-long journey and that as the teenager grows into adulthood, there will be times when the grief is reawakened and their understanding of just what has been lost deepens. I think teens tend to experience their grief more

133

I have learned a lot about myself since Bella died and it has shaped me into the person I am today. In fact, I had a dream one time that Bella came back and acted like nothing had happened. In my dream I yelled at her and told her she couldn't just act like she was dead and then come back like nothing had happened because I was now "Sarah, the girl whose sister died." I realized when I woke up that her death was such a defining moment in my life and that her death and my grief defined me as a person. I am less likely to be upset when someone has been in an accident—it's not worth it because they are *alive.*

—Sarah, fifteen

sporadically than do adults—the adults I have worked with are more willing to face their pain and to cry it out. The teens tend to show anger or feign calmness and acceptance. —**Virginia A. Simpson, Ph.D., executive director, Mourning Star Center**[4]

Teens also need to know that grief changes through the years. It will change them as well, influencing who they are in the present and affecting who they'll become in the future. It must be worked through, adapted to, and integrated into their lives, as different situations will require them to accommodate this loss again and again. They will re-visit the event continually as they grapple with its meaning—emotionally, socially, economically and spiritually—and as they struggle to find a place for their dead loved one in their present and future life. —**Marty Tousley, Hospice of the Valley, Phoenix, Arizona**[5]

Stay open—question life's uncertainty and the unknown—the ability to deal with both is a life art. Coming to terms with the truth (capital T) that nothing and no one lasts forever; that suffering exists; and that to be fully present we need to integrate these truths. . . .

Talk about feelings, images, fears, angers. Tell your story as often as you need—use as many creative outlets to tell your story (writing, painting, music, dance, etc.). . . .

Help others in any way you can—volunteer in the community perhaps even with people dealing with the same loss. —**Deborah Coryell, Good Grief**[6]

Here is what I would tell a teen. Find someone you trust (a teacher, school counselor, neighbor, friend, relative, clergy person, etc.) and with whom you feel comfortable talking. Talk about who died and what was special about that person. Tell about your experience with the death itself: where you were when the death occurred, what happened right afterward and what you're experiencing right now. Share any dreams you've had about your friend or loved one. Write a letter to the person who died and say whatever you need to say. Gather pictures, words and phrases from magazines and make a collage that tells a story about the person who died. Go on the Internet and find some of the sites (such as my own website at http://www.griefhealing.com) that offer information, comfort and support to those who are grieving. Learn what normal grief looks like and feels like, so you'll know that what you're experiencing is normal and that you're not alone. Think about what you need from others right now and let them know about it. People won't know what you need from them unless you tell them. —**Marty Tousley**[7]

Find an adult you can trust and [open up to that person]. . . .

Attend the funeral (any measures to get to the reality of the death, seeing the body, for example). . . .

Stay off the booze and dope even if the adults don't. . . .

Use your [friends] just for support, but don't expect them to know any more than you do. . . .

If you find yourself still suffering after a long time, seek help. [If you feel] more pain than you can stand, seek help. If numbed, seek help. If you feel life is stuck, seek help. . . .

If you simply feel fine, then that's nothing to feel guilty about. —**Kim Smith, Fellow Traveller, Bradford, England**[8]

GRIEF ISN'T THE END—IT'S THE BEGINNING

And a few last words from writers:[9]

> You take a handful of rocks and put them in a jar. Then once a week, you take one tiny pebble out of the jar and throw it away. When the jar is empty, why, you'll just about be over your grief. . . . [T]ime alone will do if you're short on rocks. —**Sharyn McCrumb**

> I still miss those I loved who are no longer with me but I find I am grateful for having loved them. The gratitude has finally conquered the loss. —**Rita Mae Brown**

> Death is not the enemy. Living in constant fear of it is. —**Norman Cousins**

> Life was meant to be lived. . . . [You] must never, for whatever reason, turn [your] back on life. —**Eleanor Roosevelt**

NOTES

1. See www.quotationspage.com.
2. See www.quotationspage.com.
3. Anita Diamant, *Saying Kaddish: How to Comfort the Dying, Bury the Dead & Mourn as a Jew* (New York: Schocken, 1998), 112.
4. Virginia A. Simpson, private e-mail correspondence.
5. Marty Tousley, private e-mail correspondence.
6. Deborah Coryell, private e-mail correspondence.
7. Marty Tousley, private e-mail correspondence.
8. Kim Smith, private e-mail correspondence.
9. See www.quotationspage.com.

9 Resources

You don't have to face your grief alone. A growing number of resources can assist you in dealing with the issues you face during bereavement. For this reason, I'm using the final chapter of *When Will I Stop Hurting?* to list people and places that can help you.

This resource guide contains two sections:

- ◎ **Organizations and associations**
- ◎ **Further reading**

ORGANIZATIONS AND ASSOCIATIONS

Many organizations can provide useful information on specific issues and problems that may arise during bereavement. Following the first set of listings (Grief and Bereavement), all other categories are in alphabetical order. (Please note: some organizations' services overlap. Also, note that some of the resources listed here are clearinghouses or umbrella organizations. They won't provide direct services to you, but they can inform you of other agencies or groups that offer such services in your community.)

Information on Grief and Bereavement

Accord Grief Management Services
1930 Bishop Lane, Suite 947
Louisville, Ky. 40218

Toll-free: 800.346.3087

Website: www.accordinc.org

Organized primarily "to get good information in to the hands of grieving people," Accord Grief Management Services distributes a variety of brochures, audiocassettes, and videotapes about loss and grief.

Beyond Indigo

Website: www.beyondindigo.com

"The goal of this company is to provide grief support, products, and services to individuals and companies who assist people who are grieving." Information on the Beyond Indigo website includes suggestions about grief support, healing after a loss, and dealing with sudden and violent death.

The Compassionate Friends

PO Box 3696

Oak Brook, Ill. 60522-3696

Phone: 630.990.0010

Fax: 630.990.0246

Toll-free: 877.969.0010

Website: www.compassionatefriends.org

"The Compassionate Friends is a national nonprofit, self-help support organization that offers friendship and understanding to bereaved parents, grandparents and siblings." Available resources include local chapters with support groups for the bereaved; educational services; and an extensive list of books and pamphlets.

The Dougy Center

Phone: 1.503.775.5683

Toll-free: 866.775.5683

Website: www.dougy.org

The mission of The Dougy Center for Grieving Children is "to provide families in Portland [Oregon] and the surrounding region with loving support in a safe place where children, teens, and their families grieving a death can share their experiences as they move through their healing process." In addition, the Dougy Center website has informative Web pages specifically for children and teenagers, plus an excellent search engine for locating bereavement resources in communities throughout the United States.

Fernside
2303 Indian Mound Avenue
Cincinnati, Ohio 45212
Phone: 513.841.1012
Fax: 513.841.1546
Website: www.fernside.org
Fernside, founded in 1986 in Cincinnati, Ohio, is a nonprofit, nondenominational organization serving grieving children and their families. The organization provides direct services only in the Cincinnati area; however, its site lists useful resources elsewhere in the U.S., both in on-line and print formats.

Grief Care, Inc.
26370 Via California
Capistrano Beach, Calif. 92624
Phone: 949.493.3918
Fax: 949.489.0880
Website: www.griefcare.info
Grief Care provides information about bereavement issues, as well as direct services to the bereaved in southern California.

Grief Healing, Inc.
Website: www.griefhealing.com
Founded and run by Martha Tousley, a grief counselor, Grief Healing offers message boards, contact information, and articles about grief.

Hospice Net
401 Bowling Avenue, Suite 51
Nashville, Tenn. 37205-5124
Website: www.hospicenet.org/index.html
Hospice Net provides information and support to patients and families facing life-threatening illnesses. Services include information about grief and about locating hospice (palliative

139

care) resources. The Hospice Net website includes pages specifically for bereaved teens.

Kara
457 Kingsley Avenue
Palo Alto, Calif. 94301
Phone: 650.321.5272
Website: www.kara-grief.org
"Kara is dedicated to providing compassionate support to those who are grieving a death or facing a life-threatening illness. Our mission is to empower all age groups to integrate grief into their lives and find the capacity to move forward with renewed hope." Kara provides direct services within the California Bay Area and informational services through the organization's website.

Living/Dying Project
PO Box 357
Fairfax, Calif. 94978-0357
Phone: 415.456.3915
Website: www.livingdying.org
The Living/Dying Project offers spiritual support for persons facing life-threatening illness and for those who care for them, as well as educational services. "Our programs are offered in Marin County [California] and our client services are free of charge. Educational services and training are available nationwide and internationally to health care providers and the general public."

The Mourning Star Center, Inc.
PO Box 1983
Palm Desert, Calif. 92261
Phone: 760.836.0360
Website: www.mourningstar.org
The Mourning Star Center is a nonprofit support center for grieving children and families. The Mourning Star Center provides loving support in a safe place where grieving children can share their experience as they move through their healing process. The Mourning Star Center extends supportive services

to the family, caregivers, schools, and the community. "We also receive numerous phone calls each week from parents, teachers, school counselors or other family members in Riverside County and San Bernardino County seeking help or advice in dealing with a grieving child or children."

The Shiva Foundation
Toll-free: 800.720.9544
Website: www.goodgrief.org
The Shiva Foundation is a not-for-profit, nonsectarian organization committed to developing resources and offering support in the grieving process. These programs are offered to individuals, families, and communities. On-line resources include books, links to other sites, and information about grief. The Shiva Foundation also provides phone counseling to the bereaved on a fee basis.

The Sibling Connection
www.counselingstlouis.net
The Sibling Connection is a resource site for "siblings who lost a brother or sister during childhood, adolescence, or adulthood. The issues are somewhat different for each age group. Here you will find lists of books about sibling loss, articles about the healing process, about ongoing connectedness with deceased siblings, and information about the long-term effects of early sibling loss." Resources include on-line articles, a bibliography, and a list of links to related sites.

Teen Age Grief, Inc. (TAG)
PO Box 220034
Newhall, Calif. 91322-0034
Phone: 661.253.1932
Fax: 661.253.1932
Website: www.smartlink.net/~tag/index.html
Teen Age Grief, Inc. is a nonprofit organization that provides expertise in providing grief support to bereaved teens.

Web Healing
149 Little Quarry Mews

Gaithersburg, Md. 20878
Phone: 301.670.1027
Website: www.webhealing.com

This site is a place where men and women can discuss grief-related issues, chat, or simply browse to understand and honor the many different paths to heal strong emotions. Information includes articles about grief, links to other bereavement sites, and pages for discussion. Tom Golden, a psychotherapist, also provides in-person or phone consultations on a fee basis.

Alcohol and Drug Abuse

Al-Anon Family Group Headquarters, Inc. and Alateen
PO Box 862, Midtown Station
New York, N.Y. 10018-0862
Phone: 212.302.7240
Toll-free: 800.356.9996
Toll-free: 888.4AL.ANON
Website: www.al-anon.alateen.org

Al-Anon maintains thirty thousand regional groups that serve "relatives and friends of individuals with an alcohol problem. In addition, Al-Anon produces publications, including newsletters, about alcoholism. Alateen is an organization similar to Al-Anon but focused on helping teenage friends and relatives of persons coping with alcoholism.

Cocaine Anonymous World Services
3740 Overland Avenue, Suite H
Los Angeles, Calif. 90034-6337
Phone: 310.559.5833
Toll-free: 800.347.8998
Website: www.ca.org

Cocaine Anonymous is a "fellowship of men and women who share their experiences, strength, and hope" to "solve their common problem and help others recover from addiction and remain free from cocaine and other mind-altering drugs."

National Association for Children of Alcoholics
11426 Rockville Pike, Suite 100

Rockville, Md. 20852
Phone: 301.468.0985
Website: www.nacoa.org
NACOA "supports and serves as a resource for individuals of all age groups who are COAs."

Food and Nutrition

National Association for Anorexia Nervosa and
    Associated Disorders
PO Box 7
Highland Park, Ill. 60035
Phone: 847.831.3438
Fax: 847.433.4632
Website: www.anad.org

Health Issues

Cool Nurse
Website: www.coolnurse.com
A large website with lots of data on many topics—first aid, mental health, fitness, nutrition, sexuality, bereavement, safety, male health, female health, and so forth—with abundant information.

Medline—Teen Health
National Institutes of Health
Website: www.nlm.nih.gov/medlineplus/teenhealth.html
The National Institutes of Health maintains a comprehensive website with information on many topics, including health data for teenagers. Topics include developmental issues, depression, grief, sexual health, nutrition, and mental health.

Teen Growth
Website: www.teengrowth.com
A searchable website with categories such as emotions, dealing with doctors, friendship, sports, dangers to teens, depression, grief, school issues, family matters, and sex.

143

TeensHealth
Website: www.teenshealth.org/teen/index2.html
A health-oriented website for teens with articles on physical and mental health, food and fitness, diseases and conditions, staying safe, and so forth.

TeenHealthFX
Website: www.teenhealthfx.com
The purpose of TeenHealthFX and its associated Web pages is to provide teens with access to a wide range of health and medical information. Resources range from data about specific health issues to "Teen Tips," a sequence of Web pages completely developed by teens who work on the TeenHealthFX Teen Advisory Committee.

Self-Help

Thousands of self-help groups exist to help people deal with a multitude of issues. Rather than list a sampling of these organizations, I suggest that you contact this organization to assist you in locating the group you need:

National Self-Help Clearinghouse
Graduate School and University Center
City University of New York
365 5th Avenue, Suite 3300
New York, N.Y. 10016
Phone: 212.817.1822
Website: www.selfhelpweb.org
NSHC "encourages and conducts training activities, carries out research, maintains a data bank to provide information about self-help groups, and publishes manuals, training materials, and a newsletter."

Care of Aging or Sick Parents

Children of Aging Parents
Woodbourne Office Campus, Suite 302A

1609 Woodbourne Road
Levittown, Pa. 19057-1511
Phone: 215.945.6900
Toll-free: 800.CAPS.294
Website: www.caps4caregivers.org

Suicide Prevention and Counseling

Suicide Awareness Voices of Education (SAVE)
7317 Cahill Road, Suite 207
Minneapolis, Minn. 55439-0507
Phone: 952.946.7998
Toll-free: 888.511.SAVE
E-mail Address: save@winternet.com
Website: www.save.org
This organization provides information about the causes and prevention of suicide. The website includes on-line articles on depression, danger signs of suicide, and listings of suicide resources and hotlines.

American Association of Suicidology
4201 Connecticut Avenue, N.W.
Washington, D.C. 20008
Phone: 202.237.2280
Website: www.suicidology.org
AAS can supply information about support groups for survivors of suicide, as well as literature about suicide and its aftermath for families. (Note: AAS is an information clearinghouse, not a crisis center.)

Ray of Hope
PO Box 2323
Iowa City, Iowa 52244
Phone: 319.337.9890
Ray of Hope is a self-help organization offering support for coping with suicide, loss, and grief. Services include the sale of publications and videos.

Samaritans
500 Commonwealth Avenue
Kenmore Square
Boston, Mass. 02215
Website: www.metanoia.org/suicide/index.html
This nonreligious group offers information, intervention, and publications regarding suicide. The Samaritans provide confidential emotional support to any person who is suicidal or despairing. Trained volunteers provide this free service 24 hours each day.

Violence

National Domestic Violence Hotline
Toll-free: 800.799.SAFE (7233)
Website: www.ndvh.org
Crisis intervention, information about domestic violence and referrals to local service providers to victims of domestic violence and those calling on their behalf. Hotline advocates are available to provide assistance either in English or Spanish. Volunteers have access to translators in 139 languages. Referral information is available for residents of all 50 states.

The National Organization for Victim Assistance (NOVA)
1730 Park Road, N.W.
Washington, D.C. 20010
Toll-free: 800.try.nova
Phone: 202.232.6682
Website: www.try-nova.org
NOVA is a private, nonprofit organization providing four services: national advocacy for victims' rights; direct services, including counseling and follow-up assistance for crime victims; professional development of local programs; and membership communication and support. Among other things, NOVA can help you locate victim assistance resources in your community. NOVA also provides a 24-hour telephone crisis line for all types of crime victims.

FURTHER READING

What follows is a selection of books that may be useful in the aftermath of a loved one's death. Inevitably, there's some overlap of subjects among them.

Ainley, Rosa, ed. *Death of a Mother: Daughters' Stories.* London: HarperCollins, 1994. (A compendium of essays and memoirs in which women reflect on their mothers' lives and deaths.)

Akner, Lois F. *How to Survive the Loss of a Parent: A Guide for Adults.* New York: Quill/William Morrow, 1993. (A psychotherapist's recommendations for coping with the death of a parent.)

Ascher, Barbara L. *Landscape without Gravity: A Memoir of Grief.* New York: Viking Penguin, 1994. (A personal account of coping with grief.)

Barrett, Terence. *Life after Suicide: A Survivor's Grief Experience.* Minneapolis, Minn.: Prairie House, 1989. (A personal account of coping with the aftermath of suicide.)

Bernstein, Joanne E. *Loss.* New York: Clarion Books, 1977. (Concise, clear advice on dealing with loss and bereavement.)

Bloomfield, Harold H. *Making Peace with Your Parents.* New York: Random House, 1983. (A self-help manual for adults in conflict with their parents.)

Bowlby, John. *Attachment and Loss.* Vol. 3, *Loss.* New York: Basic Books, 1980. (An English psychiatrist's ground-breaking study of loss and grief.)

Caine, Lynn. *Lifelines.* New York: Doubleday, 1978. (The problem of loneliness and how to overcome it.)

Canfield, Jack. *Chicken Soup for the Teenage Soul on Tough Stuff: Stories of Tough Times and Lessons Learned.* New York: Health Communications, 2001. (Inspirational stories about teenagers coping with life's uncertainties and challenges, including depression, loss, and grief.)

Cobain, Bev. *When Nothing Matters Anymore: A Survival Guide for Depressed Teens.* Minneapolis, Minn.: Free Spirit, 2000. (Stories, tips, and resources for teenagers struggling with depression.)

Colgrove, Melba, et al. *How to Survive the Loss of a Love.* Los Angeles: Prelude, 1991. (Advice, meditations, and poems about dealing with grief.)

Gootman, Marilyn E. *When a Friend Dies: A Book for Teens about Grieving and Healing.* Minneapolis, Minn.: Free Spirit, 1994. (Inspirational thoughts for dealing with loss and grief.)

Grollman, Earl, ed. *Concerning Death: A Practical Guide for the Living.* Boston: Beacon, 1974. (Comprehensive guide to issues of death and loss.)

——. *Living When a Loved One Has Died.* Boston: Beacon, 1974. (Reassuring essays about coping with loss.)

——. *Straight Talk about Death for Teenagers: How to Cope with Losing Someone You Love.* Boston: Beacon, 1993. (Personal essays about death, loss, and grief.)

——. *Suicide: Prevention, Intervention, and Post-Intervention.* Boston: Beacon, 1988. (Recommendations for dealing with suicide and its aftermath.)

——. *What Helped Me When My Loved One Died.* Boston: Beacon, 1981. (More essays about bereavement by a well-known writer on death and dying.)

Henderson, Diane. *Coping with Grief.* Tuscumbia, Ala.: Henderson Clark, 1979. (A short booklet about the grief process.)

Kennedy, Alexandra. *Losing a Parent: Passage to a New Way of Living.* San Francisco: Harper San Francisco, 1991. (A psychotherapist's insights into coping with a parent's death.)

Koman, Aleta. *How to Mend a Broken Heart: Letting Go and Moving On.* Chicago: Contemporary Books, 1997. (Advice for coping with loss, including—but not limited to—loss resulting from a death.)

Krementz, Jill. *How It Feels When a Parent Dies.* New York: Alfred A. Knopf, 1981. (Stories of bereaved children, with photographs.)

Kübler-Ross, Elisabeth. *Death: The Final Stage of Growth.* New York: Macmillan, 1981. (Essays and photo essays about the dying.)

———.*Living with Death and Dying.* New York: Macmillan, 1981. (Essays about various issues of death and dying.)

———. *On Death and Dying.* New York: Macmillan, 1981. (A classic, popular work about understanding death and dying.)

LeShan, Eda. *Learning to Say Good-By.* New York: Avon, 1976. (A sensitive book for children about the death of parents.)

Levine, Stephen. *Healing into Life and Death.* New York: Doubleday, 1989. (Insights into illness and death as transformative experiences.)

———. *Who Dies?* New York: Anchor/Doubleday, 1989. (Similar in nature to the author's book noted above.)

Lewis, C. S. *A Grief Observed.* New York: Bantam Books, 1983. (A famous theologian's observations on loss and grief.)

Manning, Doug. *Comforting Those Who Grieve.* San Francisco: Harper San Francisco, 1987. (A minister's recommendations for dealing with grief.)

———. *Don't Take My Grief Away.* New York: Harper and Row, 1984. (Recommendations similar to those offered in the book above.)

Miller, Jack. *Healing Our Losses: A Journal for Working through Your Grief.* Boston: Resource, 1993. (A workbook approach to resolving bereavement.)

Moffat, Mary J., ed. *In the Midst of Winter: Selections from the Literature of Mourning.* New York: Random House, 1992. (An anthology of writings about grief and bereavement.)

Myers, Edward. *When Parents Die: A Guide for Adults.* New York: Penguin Books, 1997. (Advice on how to deal with the death of a parent.)

Parkes, Colin Murray. *Bereavement: Studies of Grief in Adult Life.* New York: International Universities Press, 1977. (An English psychologist's study of bereavement.)

Parkes, Colin Murray, and Robert S. Weiss. *Recovery from Bereavement.* New York: Basic Books, 1983. (A pioneering study of widowhood and its wider implications for bereavement.)

Pinkus, Lily. *Death and the Family.* New York: Vintage Books, 1974. (Family dynamics and bereavement.)

Raphael, Beverley. *The Anatomy of Bereavement.* New York: Basic Books, 1983. (An Australian psychiatrist's perceptions of loss and grief.)

Rapoport, Nessa. *Woman's Book of Grieving.* New York: William Morrow, 1994. (Advice on bereavement specifically for women.)

Sanders, Catherine. *Surviving Grief . . . and Learning to Live Again.* New York: John Wiley and Sons, 1992. (Recommendations for dealing with the grief process.)

Shephard, Martin. *Someone You Love Is Dying.* New York: Harper and Row, 1980. (Practical information about loss and grief.)

Silverstone, Barbara, and Helen Kandel Hyman. *You and Your Aging Parent.* New York: Pantheon, 1982. (An excellent guidebook for helping and dealing with elderly parents.)

Staudacher, Carol. *A Time to Grieve: Meditations for Healing after the Death of a Loved One.* San Francisco: Harper San Francisco, 1994. (Reflections for the bereaved.)

Tatelbaum, Judy. *The Courage to Grieve.* New York: Harper and Row, 1984. (Useful recommendations about dealing with grief.)

Temes, Roberta. *Living with an Empty Chair.* Amherst, Mass.: Mandala, 1977. (An unusually eloquent commentary on loss and grief.)

Vail, Elaine. *A Personal Guide to Living with Loss.* New York: John Wiley and Sons, 1982. (Comprehensive treatment, including practical matters.)

Volkan, Vamik, and Elizabeth Zintl. *Life after Loss: The Lessons of Grief.* New York: Macmillan, 1994. (The nature and process of bereavement.)

Wolfelt, Alan D. *Healing Your Grieving Heart for Teens: 100 Practical Ideas.* Fort Collins, Colo.: Companion, 2001. (A collection of short, specific recommendations for teenagers who have suffered a loss.)

Youngs, Betty B., ed. *Taste Berries for Teens: Inspirational Short Stories and Encouragement on Life, Love, Friendship, and Tough Issues.* New York: Health Communications Audio, 1999. (Inspiring stories about how teenagers can face life's difficulties and challenges.)

Glossary

Acute illness. A disease that has a sudden start, sharp increase in symptoms, and short duration

Aneurysm. An abnormal, blood-filled stretching of a blood vessel

Anticipatory grieving. A process of experiencing aspects of grief before a loss or death has actually occurred

Bereavement. Deep psychological distress caused by a loss, which may include emotions such as sadness, longing, and deprivation; generally synonymous with **grief**

Chronic illness. A disease characterized by long duration, recurrence, or gradual progression

Denial. A refusal or inability to accept the reality of a situation, such as the death of a loved one

Depression. A mental state marked by sadness, inactivity, and difficulty in thinking or concentrating

Double-bind. A psychological dilemma in which someone experiences frustrating outcomes to a situation no matter what he or she chooses to do

Endorphins. Naturally occurring molecules that attach to special receptors in the brain and spinal cord to inhibit pain signals

Grief. Deep psychological distress caused by a loss, which may include emotions such as sadness, longing, and deprivation; generally synonymous with **bereavement**

Hatha yoga. A system of stretching exercises and poses (or postures) intended to promote physical health, relaxation, and emotional stability

Hemorrhage. Abundant release of blood

Hospice. An organization designed to provide physical and emotional care to terminally ill patients

JROTC. Junior Reserve Officer Training Corps, a high school-level program for military education

Judicial. Pertaining to the court system

Lupus erythmatosis. A progressive disease characterized by damage to internal organs, skin, joints, and other body systems

Mourning. The outward customs or behavior (such as attending specific types of religious services or wearing black clothes) that express grief

Psychotherapy. The treatment of mental or emotional difficulties by means of talking or other methods

Qi gong. An ancient Chinese system that combines movement and meditation

Sitting shiva. A Jewish custom that involves a seven-day period of mourning

Survivor guilt. Feelings of guilt that some people feel when they have survived an accident or other tragedy in which others have died

T'ai chi (or **T'ai chi ch'uan**). An ancient Chinese system that combines movement and meditation

Trauma. Injury or wounds, as from an accident

Wake. A Christian custom that involves a vigil or watch over the body of a dead person prior to burial, often with prayers or singing

Index

About the Author

Edward Myers is the author of thirty published or forthcoming books. Among these are three novels (*The Mountain Made of Light, Fire and Ice,* and *The Summit*), twelve children's books (including *Duck and Cover, Ice, Climb or Die, Survival of the Fittest,* and *The Adventures of Forri the Baker*), and a well-received, much-reprinted book about bereavement—*When Parents Die: A Guide for Adults*. He has also coauthored many books. Myers lives with his wife and two children in the New York metropolitan area.

.